April 2007

Thanks for pouring your time &
prayer in your mentor relationship.
May you know the Lord's pleasure
as you continue to grow as a woman
of influence. Zephaniah 3:17!

Joy & Carrie

WOMAN *of* INFLUENCE

Ten Traits of Those Who
Want to Make a Difference

Pam Farrel

IVP Books

An imprint of InterVarsity Press
Downers Grove, Illinois

InterVarsity Press
P.O. Box 1400, Downers Grove, IL 60515-1426
World Wide Web: www.ivpress.com
E-mail: mail@ivpress.com

InterVarsity Press® is the book-publishing division of InterVarsity Christian Fellowship/USA®, a student movement active on campus at hundreds of universities, colleges and schools of nursing in the United States of America, and a member movement of the International Fellowship of Evangelical Students. For information about local and regional activities, write Public Relations Dept., InterVarsity Christian Fellowship/USA, 6400 Schroeder Rd., P.O. Box 7895, Madison, WI 53707-7895, or visit the IVCF website at <www.intervarsity.org>.

All Scripture quotations, unless otherwise indicated, are taken from the Holy Bible, New International Version®. NIV®. Copyright ©1973, 1978, 1984 by International Bible Society. Used by permission of Zondervan Publishing House. All rights reserved.

Design: Cindy Kiple
Images: Debra McClinton/Getty Images

ISBN-10: 0-8308-2362-X
ISBN-13: 978-0-8308-2362-8

Printed in the United States of America ∞

Library of Congress Cataloging-in-Publication Data

Farrel, Pam, 1959-
  Woman of influence: ten traits of those who want to make a
  difference
/ Pam Farrel. – [Rev. ed.].
    p. cm.
  Includes bibliographical references.
  ISBN-13: 978-0-8308-2362-8 (pbk.: alk. paper)
  ISBN-10: 0-8308-2362-X (pbk.: alk. paper)
  1. Women in Christianity. 2. Christian leadership. 3. Women in
  the Bible.
  I. Title.
BV639.W7F37 2006
248.8'43—dc22
                                                                2006004134

| P | 19 | 18 | 17 | 16 | 15 | 14 | 13 | 12 | 11 | 10 | 9 | 8 | 7 | 6 | 5 | 4 | 3 | 2 | 1 |
| Y | 21 | 20 | 19 | 18 | 17 | 16 | 15 | 14 | 13 | 12 | 11 | 10 | 09 | 08 | 07 | 06 |

CONTENTS

INTRODUCTION
What Is a Woman of Influence Like?

A young woman is walking along the beach. She sees an older woman picking up beached starfish and tossing them back into the sea. The young woman asks, "Why are you doing that? There are so many starfish, and the waves keep washing them up on shore. You toss a few back, but what difference does it make?"

The older woman picks up a starfish, flings it into the ocean and says, "It made a difference to *that* one!"

DO YOU WANT TO MAKE A DIFFERENCE?

My desire is to equip women to be all God intends them to be. For many years I studied the women in the Bible, searching for the qualities that made them usable to God. Then I started to observe contemporary women whose lives were making a difference in the world to which God had called them—government, religion, the arts, business, education, medicine, science, social service and the home. I noticed that all these women had certain character qualities in common. As I read biographies of women who have influenced history, I saw similar character traits.

Influence can be defined as *earning the right to be heard so that others are moved toward their best.* While success is often "I" oriented, influence is "other" oriented. We earn the privilege of influencing another person's life. We are better equipped for influence if we develop the ten traits, or character qualities, set forth in this book.

You may think, *Ten traits! Oh, no, pack my bags, I'm going on a guilt trip! I can't be all those things.* This book is *not* about guilt; it's about growth. Influence does not require perfection on our part; it requires faithfulness to God's call.

When I was a little girl, I loved to pick dandelions when they were fluffy and white. I'd blow, and hundreds of seeds would fly into the air. I tried to watch where they all went, but most of them blew higher and higher until they disappeared. Just like those seeds, influence often goes unseen until it blossoms later in the garden of someone else's life.

> *Influence can be defined as earning the right to be heard so that others are moved toward their best.*

My mother told me from early on, "Pam, be a leader." Even now during my darkest days, I can hear her whisper, "You can do it. Just try. You'll see. I know you can."

My grandmother's words, spoken during dishwashing conversations, always reminded me of my purpose: "Pam, share your talent." My grandmother would take me to a nursing home where I would do gymnastics for the residents. Then together we would give away fruit and kind words.

THE SEEDS OF INFLUENCE IN MY LIFE

Kathy Hansell and her eight-year-old daughter Kelly let me play in their front yard and encouraged my family to go to church. That influence eventually led me into the Bible, where I met Jesus personally.

My sister Deney was my best friend through our growing up years. Night after night we whispered hopes and dreams in the shadows of our cozy room. My sisters-in-law Erin and Kathy, though younger, are often wiser than I am. When I married Bill, I gained a sister in Lori, whose practical wisdom has encouraged me to step into bigger and broader arenas.

In college, Tina, a young newlywed on staff with Campus Crusade for Christ, and her mentor, Faith, taught me about growing in my walk with God. Grace, Cindy and Debbie, my courageous peers in the group, encouraged me to walk the new life.

In seminary, Phoebe taught me graciousness and hospitality and instilled in me a deeper hunger to reach the lost. Karen prayed for me and encouraged me to be myself. Sally and her husband, Jim, believed God had a calling on my life, so they passed the writing baton in a mentoring relationship.

Like salt shaken out, influence is hard to see, but its flavor is impossible to miss.

My kindred friends involved with women's ministry have held me up with their prayers. Many other women have buoyed me up in times of weariness and stress. Some will be on the pages of this book, but all are on the pages of my heart. Like salt shaken out, influence is hard to see, but its flavor is impossible to miss.

The women who influenced me had no way of knowing how God used them. You may feel the same way. You want to be used by God but have no idea how. Or you feel God has given you a platform to make a difference and you want to make the best use of it. It is my prayer that within the pages of this book you will discover the hope, strength and encouragement to be a "woman of influence" within your world.

The shores of your life are covered with starfish. Make a difference.

I

IMPASSIONED
Finding Your Unique Calling

Heat is required to forge anything.
Every great accomplishment is the story of a flaming heart.

MARY LOU RETTON

*I*ndia was the last place this teenage girl wanted to be. Ida's parents were missionaries, but soon she would be old enough to choose her future for herself. She would escape India and return to the States forever.

One night three men came knocking at her father's door. They knew he was a doctor. "Can you help our wives?" they asked. The visitors explained that the women were in labor and having a difficult time. The doctor ran for his bag, but the men stopped him. They explained that he couldn't come. It would not be right in their culture for a man to have this kind of contact with a woman. There was no one else, and so the men left.

Ida's heart was shot through with pangs of grief. These women had endured nine months of pregnancy, yet they would probably never hold their newborns in their arms. She tried in vain to sleep.

I could not sleep that night—it was too terrible. Within the very touch of my hand were three young girls dying because there was no woman to help them. I spent much of the night in anguish and prayer. I did not want to spend my life in India. My friends were begging me to return to the joyous opportunities of a young girl in America. I went to bed in the early morning after praying for much guidance. I think that was the first time I ever met God face to face, and all that time it seemed He was calling me into this work. Early in the morning I heard the "tom tom" beating in the village and it struck terror in my heart, for it was a death message.

One heart impassioned by God can make a difference.

Ida left India. Many years later I shared Ida's story when I was speaking. Afterward a woman came running up to me and said, "You just have to know!"

"What do I have to know?" I asked her.

"I grew up in India. My parents were both medical doctors and they served at the Ida Scudder Memorial Hospital!"

Ida did leave India—for her medical studies in 1895. And a few years later Dr. Ida Scudder returned with a medical degree and a thousand-dollar check to begin her work among the women of India. Soon other women followed her to help with the cause. Decades later Ida's legacy lives on! One heart impassioned by God can make a difference.

That's how passion is born: God calls you and says, "Look. This is a need." You see the need, you know you can fill the need—and deep in your heart you know your life will never be the same. A passionate call happens when the world's great need meets your deep desire and connects with God's infinite power.

PASSION PLANTED

We do not have to go in search of passion. Instead we need to search for God, who plants the seed of passion in our hearts. When we seek to be intimately connected with him, he will use the desires of our heart, the circumstances of our life and his confirming Word to solidify and reveal our passion.

Passion is a gift from God to empower you.

In the Bible, God sometimes told parents that their children were to accomplish a special work. The parents of John the Baptist were told, "Many of the people of Israel will he bring back to the Lord their God. And he will . . . make ready a people prepared for the Lord" (Luke 1:16-17). The Lord told Jeremiah, "Before I formed you in the womb I knew you, before you were born I set you apart; I appointed you as a prophet to the nations" (Jeremiah 1:4-5).

Passion is a gift from God to empower you. Passion is pure motivation sent through pure means to accomplish pure results that will glorify God and meet the needs of people. The method of an impassioned heart may change or adapt over time, but the passion remains constant.

For example, you may be passionate about caring for needy and hurting people. Your passion may lead you into nursing, administrating a nonprofit organization, volunteering in a service organization, launching a ministry in your local church or creating a business that fills a niche for needy people. Same passion, different methods.

PURE MOTIVATION

As a college freshman I was confidently going nowhere. From the outside it appeared I had all I needed—a scholarship, grades, friends, a boyfriend—but inside I was struggling with huge issues. *Why am I here? What difference can I make?* I had been racking up awards trying to validate myself, but I was afraid I wouldn't be able to keep hauling in those awards. In order to gain acceptance, I felt pressure to give my heart and my sexuality away. I didn't want to. And I didn't want to live on the treadmill of acquisitions anymore. That's when a friend invited me to a Bible study. Appropriately, my friend's name was Grace!

At the Bible study I learned about the God I had met when I was eight years old. I learned about his unconditional love and the plan he had for me to give me a future and a hope. In the course of a year, I was a new person. I felt free to choose the best God had for me. I felt free to excel at whatever God placed in front of me and not worry about the rest. And I was no longer driven by fear. My high school sweetheart and I parted as friends. I started to gain a clearer picture of who I was and what the future might hold.

PURE MEANS

A few months later, at a leadership conference for college students, a speaker challenged us to ask God what his plans were for our lives. I found a quiet spot and began running my options past God: A congresswoman, Lord? A public relations executive? A TV anchorwoman? A teacher?

Silence.

Then God reminded me of a prayer I had prayed as a nine-year-old girl. The prayer went like this: "God, if you can arrange it, I'd really like to marry a pastor. I like the families of the pastors and missionaries I've met. And I want to tell people how they can have you for a best friend, just like you and me, God. Okay? But whether I marry a pastor or not, I want to serve you."

I told God that I agreed with the prayer I had prayed as a young girl. I made a commitment to investigate how I might use my gifts and talents in a full-time Christian career. I knew it might still be his will that I serve in the secular arena, but I had to be open to the option of ministry as a career.

Over the course of several years, I developed a passion for a ministry of encouraging women to become all they were created to be. God would place a young woman before me. I would disciple her. He would bring another. I would disciple her. Then one day while I was sharing an evangelistic booklet with a student, a young woman ran up to us screaming, "Listen to her. Listen to her. She knows what she's talking about!"

I recognized this enthusiastic woman as my next-door neighbor from the dorm a few years earlier. She went on, "I lived in the dorm with Pam. I was in a Bible study with her—well, that is, when I came—and she told me all this stuff about God. I didn't listen then, but last year I realized Jesus was the answer I'd been looking for. My life is totally different. I'm happy for the first time in my life. It works!"

PURE RESULTS

It works! It works! Those words rang in my head. I kept discipling and sharing Christ. A few years later, the thank-you notes began to arrive. I was finishing my education. I had continued to disciple others during those years. Now I had to decide what I wanted to do with my future. I took the afternoon off, closed myself away in an office and prayed.

The Holy Spirit did an "It's a Wonderful Life" type of review for me. I realized afresh that God had made a radical difference in my life. One after another, he brought to mind girls and women who had been encouraged through my ministry. *You were my tool to show this one that she had an artistic gift to share. You were my tool to train this one*

*in ministry, and she's gone on to do great things for me. You were my tool
to get this girl off welfare and out of an abusive relationship. This one is off
drugs. This one is alive and not suicidal. This marriage is saved. This one
finished college. This one went into missions . . .*

I sat in tears, humbled by the fact that God had used me. I realized
I was propelled by a passion deep in my heart. I did a quick review
of the women leaders I greatly respect: writers, speakers, parachurch
staff, teachers, professors, directors of women's ministries. I noticed
they all had one thing in common—they had carried the gospel to
their generation. Was I willing to carry the gospel to *my* generation?

Yes, Lord.

For some of you reading this book, God will be asking, "Are you
willing to commit yourself full time to my ministry?" For others, God
will ask, "In your already busy life, are you willing to take up a cause?
Will you mentor a young woman, help that single mom? Are you
willing to take on that Sunday school class, that group of younger
moms, those teen girls, those immigrant women or those victims of
domestic violence or a prostitute or a runaway? Are you afraid? Are
you at least willing to be made willing to make a difference?"

Are you willing to be impassioned by God and have a heart set
aflame with his love? Simply pray, "God, I am willing. Impassion my
heart."

FEAR OF PASSION

You may be reluctant to be impassioned. You may fear the unknown.
You may fear the responsibility of carrying the burden. You may fear
burnout from caring too much. You may feel inadequate or unpre-
pared to carry the passion.

My biggest struggle with my own passion is that at times it feels
too big. I sometimes feel as if I carry the world like a heart-shaped
locket around my neck. How can I be numb to the 23 million refu-

gees, three-quarters of them women and children, who flee war, rape, violence and hunger? How can I stand idle when in India and China there are 77 million fewer women than there should be because of sex-selection abortions?

An ad in India said it is better to spend $38 now on an abortion than $3800 later on a dowry. The dowry system, once a celebration showering money and gifts on a new couple, has grown into a blackmail system by which a prospective husband demands a dowry or threatens not to marry. After the marriage, the demands keep coming. If the demands are not met, the bride may be set on fire by her new husband, who often claims that she died in a kitchen accident. According to the Indian Ministry of Home Affairs and the National Crime Records Bureau, there were 6,285 deaths in India related to dowry demands in 2003.

Each year two million girls worldwide are at risk of female circumcision, or genital mutilation. Some die; some become infertile; many experience long-term health complications. In developing countries, two girls out of five get no education, even though a mother's educational level is the key factor in lowering child mortality rates. Studies have shown that each year a mother is educated reduces infant mortality by 5 to 10 percent. How can I sit idle when my sisters in Muslim countries may not be allowed to learn to read? How can I enjoy a refrigerator packed with food when many mothers and girls are starving?

The white picket fences of the United States are by no means stopping injustice. Domestic problems include battered women, undereducated women, substance abuse, depression, suicide and much more! Between 1970 and 2003 the number of out-of-wedlock births has increased from 11 percent of live births to 35 percent. The divorce rate quadrupled while the number of children living in single-parent homes tripled. Teen suicide rose 200 percent, and SAT scores plummeted.

And the children! According to Children of the Night, "International Relief Organizations suggest there are 300,000 children working as prostitutes in the U.S. It is estimated that somewhere between one and one half million children run away from home each year. It is safe to estimate that about one-third of those children have some type of involvement with prostitution and/or pornography." The average age of Nepalese girls entering an Indian brothel is said to be 10-14 years. There are approximately 200,000 women and children missing in Nepal who are believed to have been trafficked to India. The government of India estimated that 30 percent of all prostitutes were below the age of twenty. UNICEF estimates that 1.2 million children are trafficked worldwide each year.

And these are only a few issues. What about the porn trade, adult prostitution, world hunger, victims of natural disasters, HIV/AIDS or simply poverty?

In addition to external circumstances, people's brokenness sometimes leads them to make horrific choices, which continue the cycle of pain. One mother drowns her two preschool boys in a lake; another fakes a kidnapping. Teachers who are supposed to protect and educate are having affairs with their students—some as young as sixth grade! And think of all the women who live far below their potential just because someone along the way told them they were stupid, ugly or untalented. So many people need to hear of God's love for them. George Barna did a study on what Americans believe and discovered that in the U.S. two-thirds haven't understood God in a way they can respond to. There are millions of broken hearts, broken homes, broken lives and broken dreams.

Feeling overwhelmed? So am I. The needs are so great that we want to bury our heads in the sands of apathy. However, if we are willing, God will help us engage the world around us. We can experience the amazing opportunity of literally saving a life, if we will open up our hearts, homes and schedules, one person, one hour, one small opportunity at a time.

PASSION IN THE REAL WORLD

One afternoon I was driving to meet my husband for dinner. My small children were in the back seat of my car. It was a chilly afternoon, and the overcast clouds made all of life seem gray. I drove down a residential street near an elementary school. To my left, I saw a young man and woman arguing. There was fear in the woman's face. The man began to push her, then hit her. The street was full of cars, but no one stopped.

My heart was screaming to my head. *She could be battered! She could be raped! He has to be stopped!* The man was now trying to force the woman into a car. I pulled over next to the car, slammed on my brakes, rolled down my window and yelled, "Leave her alone—right now! I'm going to phone the police, so you'd better let her go and get out of here!" The young woman broke free and raced toward a nearby home.

By this time I had caused a traffic jam, so I quickly pulled back onto the road and turned the corner. Another driver pulled to the side of the road and waved to me. "Is she okay?" she asked. Then she offered to call the police on her phone.

Just then another car pulled up behind us. I suddenly remembered that a gang shooting had occurred on this block just a few weeks before! Was the angry man coming after me? I sighed with relief when I saw it was another woman. She pulled up next to me and lowered her window. "Thought I'd let you know that girl got into the house, and her boyfriend—or whatever—sped away in his car."

"Thanks," I said.

"You bet. I saw it too, but I didn't know what to do."

I swallowed my pounding heart that seemed to be beating its way up my throat. "I know—I just prayed and reacted!" The woman with the phone came back and said the police had received a 911 call from the house and were on their way.

I drove away. From the back seat my three-year-old said, "Mom, do you think that man has a gun and will come shoot us?" Then I started to cry.

God, he could have shot us. He could have pulled out a gun and shot at me and hit one of my babies instead! But if that had been my daughter, I would have wanted someone to do what I did. This burden is so heavy, God. If I see injustice, I just act. Guard my family. Give me wisdom. I'm asking you to bridle this passion when it needs to bridled and unleash it with all its fury when it needs to be unleashed.

PASSION BOOMERANGS BACK TO BLESS

Passion is like a love boomerang. When you live out your God-given passion, God will boomerang blessings back into your own heart, life and family. One vivid example is my relationship with Lisa.

Passion is like a love boomerang.

Lisa entered my life when her next-door neighbor Joanna brought her and her husband to church. Joanna realized that things were not great on the home front for Lisa. Soon afterward, Lisa's husband became so violent that the police were called. Then he left her for another woman, leaving Lisa as the single mom of a two-year-old. I took Lisa under my wing and helped her rebuild her life and her family and begin a ministry to other single mothers. She wanted to avoid any more emotional pain, so I was part of a group of friends who "interviewed" her potential dates to sift out the unhealthy men. Eventually Lisa did meet a precious man. We walked them through premarital counseling, and my husband preformed the ceremony.

Later Lisa and her family moved away. But God wouldn't let her off my heart. I'd call her, pray for her, send her resources. Then one morning I awoke early in an unexplainable panic for Lisa. I called her. No answer. I called her husband at work. I found out that Lisa was so sick in her pregnancy that she was hospitalized. Her husband had come home to discover her passed out on the floor, near death.

The experience cemented our friendship because I had to make numerous calls to find her, and I continued to call her to encourage her through that trial, then through her husband's health crisis with cancer, a move, and her husband's unemployment for a season. Then my husband wrote her husband a letter of recommendation for a job at a church, and they went on staff. I walked alongside her as she developed You Can! Ministries and launched her speaking ministry.

Then one day, years later, my own life began to unravel. A health issue forced my husband to make a job change. We struggled financially. I was afraid I would to lose Bill to his health crisis, and I had to work long hours to provide for the family. I was emotionally and physically exhausted. And Lisa picked me up. She prayer walked with me weekly. Unknown to me, she fasted regularly for a year on our behalf. Then she told us of a job opening at her church that was perfect for my husband—and her husband recommended mine!

Love always boomerangs back. Passion is not "I'll scratch your back, you scratch mine," but giving yourself fully to God and trusting the results to him. Sometimes you receive a deep sense of personal satisfaction knowing your life counted in the life of another. Other times you won't even know the fruit this side of heaven, but the sense of God smiling at your obedience is reward enough for your soul.

PASSION PROTECTED

She was young and beautiful. Heads turned when she entered a room. She was married to a powerful, rich man, and life seemed perfect. Perfect—except for a secret that she kept hidden from everyone, including her husband. Only her family knew who she really was.

Then one day she heard of a plot that would harm her family, her culture and her future. The leader of a radical extremist group had gained the confidence of her husband and arranged for the wholesale slaughter of her entire people. She was safe—the secret of her ethnic identity hadn't gotten out—but others were in danger. Her perfect life was crumbling before her eyes. What should she do?

She received a stealth visit from her uncle. After he left, his words rang in her heart. "Who knows, maybe you have come to this position for such a time as this." She promised her uncle that she would go to her husband on behalf of her people. Her secret would be out. Her life would be on the line. What could she do?

The young woman was Esther in the Bible, and she gives us the answer for how to handle fear:

> Then Esther told them to reply to Mordecai, "Go, assemble all the Jews who are found in Susa, and fast for me; do not eat or drink for three days, night or day. I and my maidens also will fast in the same way. And thus I will go in to the king, which is not according to the law; and if I perish, I perish." (Esther 4:16 NASB)

Esther did not perish. She and her people were saved. Esther was transformed from a timid trembler to a passionate princess by God's passion planted within her through the power of her friends' prayers. God takes care of his impassioned people.

If fear is holding you back from answering God's call on your life, ask someone near you to pray with you. Today I am not nearly so afraid because I have seen God carrying the burden for the passion he placed within me. He sends the people, resources, wisdom and tangible help to carry the passion he has given me.

PASSION ON HOLD

It seems strange when it happens, but God will sometimes fill your heart with passion and then make you wait. At times, his purpose for your life is best accomplished when he puts your passion on hold.

My husband and I felt called to full-time Christian work, but God did not allow us to jump in as soon as we planned. I worked and put Bill through an undergraduate program while we both volunteered in youth ministry. We looked forward to graduation and going right into youth ministry full time. Then a colleague suggested that, since we wanted a lifelong professional ministry, it would be wise to invest in seminary training. My heart was a mixture of humble obedience and broken dreams. I cried all night in God's waiting room. I didn't know how to put my passion on hold. More schooling meant more waiting, and I was tired of waiting.

God's apparent leading was hard for us to accept. We counseled with the associate pastor of our church. This gracious man pointed out to us that God, having placed his calling in us, was holding us back so our passion would build, much as a glowing ember can grow into a blazing fire. He explained that God was ensuring that our passion would be strong enough to carry us through even the toughest of times. Sitting in God's waiting room transformed our passion into a sacrificial attitude of *whatever it takes, Lord.*

Passion Unfurled

God is the master of calling the unlikely to do the impossible. Out of pain, he creates a platform.

Sojourner Truth was an ex-slave turned evangelist when women and African Americans couldn't even vote, let alone preach. She simply told her own story of faith. Here is the account of her appearance at the 1851 Women's Rights Convention in Akron, Ohio.

Sojourner walked to the podium and slowly took off her sunbonnet. Her six-foot frame towered over the audience. She began to speak in her deep, resonant voice: "Well, children, where there is so much racket, there must be something out of kilter, I think between the Negroes of the South and the women of the North—all talking about rights—the white men will be in a fix pretty soon. But what's all this talking about?"

Sojourner pointed to one of the ministers. "That man over there says that women need to be helped into carriages, and lifted over ditches, and to have the best place everywhere. Nobody helps me any best place. And ain't I a woman?"

Sojourner raised herself to her full height. "Look at me! Look at my arm." She bared her right arm and flexed her powerful muscles. "I have plowed, I have planted and I have gathered into barns. And no man could head me. And ain't I a woman?"

"I could work as much, and eat as much as man—when I could get it—and bear the lash as well! And ain't I a woman? I have borne children and seen most of them sold into slavery, and when I cried out with a mother's grief, none but Jesus heard me. And ain't I a woman?"

The women in the audience began to cheer wildly.

She pointed to another minister. "He talks about this thing in the head. What's that they call it?"

"Intellect," whispered a woman nearby.

"That's it, honey. What's intellect got to do with women's rights or black folks' rights? If my cup won't hold but a pint and yours holds a quart, wouldn't you be mean not to let me have my little half-measure full?

"That little man in black there! He says women can't have as much rights as men. 'Cause Christ wasn't a woman." She stood with outstretched arms and eyes of fire. "Where did your Christ come from?"

"*Where did your Christ come from?*" she thundered again. "From God and a Woman! Man had nothing to do with him!"

The entire church now roared with deafening applause.

"If the first woman God ever made was strong enough to turn the world upside down all alone, these women together ought to be able to turn it back and get it right-side up again."

God took Sojourner Truth's pain over all those years and turned it into a pulpit of truth. Her passion propelled her past human obstacles into the center of God's will.

THE ROOTS OF PASSION

The passion we are talking about is not just a feeling. We act on feelings when it is convenient. We *must* act on passion! Convictions give staying power to passion.

We act on feelings when it is convenient. We must act on passion!

To discover what you are truly passionate about, ask yourself a few key questions:

- When the house is quiet, where do your daydreams take you?

- What was the last issue that made you righteously angry, or brought you to tears?

- When you read God's Word, are there common themes in the verses you mark?

- What breaks your heart?

- What do you talk about the most?

- What truths would you die for?

- What principles or beliefs would you go to jail to protect?

- What people would you place your neck on the chopping block for? And why would you do it?

- Who and what would you be inconvenienced for day after day?

PASSION TO DIE FOR

Many women sail through their entire lives never faced with a life-and-death decision. We in the Western world can easily give lip service to various causes and principles. We may *hope* that if it came right down to it we would say, "I would rather die than break my faith." Those were the words Ann Askew actually spoke to the Lord Chancellor in the tumult of the Reformation. She was one of many brave women burned at the stake for their Christian beliefs.

When A. Wetherell Johnson was a young missionary in China, she led a young woman to faith in Christ. The young woman began to attend a Bible study group. One morning she told Miss Johnson, "After yesterday afternoon, I decided I would never again worship idols." The custom in this woman's home, as in most homes in China at the time, was to bow before the house idol each morning before leaving for school or work. She was the youngest of twelve children, and when it was finally her turn, she stood up straight and said, "I worship Jesus and I cannot bow down to the idol." Her mother and father tried to talk her into complying. When she would not give in, her father took her out and beat her unmercifully. She still refused to worship the idol.

When the girl recounted the story to Miss Johnson, Miss Johnson began to weep. But the young woman said, "Don't cry, Teacher. The Lord was with me just as he was with the three Israelites in the fire, and he has taken the sting away."

Over the centuries many courageous women have died for their faith. One of the first recorded women martyrs was Perpetua in the early third century. We know her through her writings and the accounts of eyewitnesses.

Perpetua was born to a wealthy family, and she had a slave about her same age, Felicitas. These two young mothers had come to faith in Christ and refused to renounce their faith in him. They were stripped and thrown into an arena with a mad cow. Even the bloodthirsty crowds at the coliseum were aghast at the sight of a new mother, breasts dripping with milk, thrown naked into such a pit. So the two were recalled, given loosely fitting gowns and sent back out. Perpetua was hit first and knocked to the ground. She sat up and, seeing that her gown had been torn, fumbled with the fabric to maintain her modesty. She stopped to clip back her hair because she thought it not proper that a martyr be disheveled. She stood to her feet. She saw Felicitas, bruised and broken, and ran to help her. Becoming impatient, the crowd demanded that the two women be brought out into the open and die by the sword. Perpetua and Felicitas voluntarily moved out to the center of the arena.

The gladiators silently sliced into the martyrs. Perpetua groaned as the sword plunged into her side. She lifted her head, took the trembling hand of the gladiator and pointed to her throat. Perpetua chose to die for the One who had died for her.

I want to think I would be brave like Perpetua and Felicitas. But what does it mean to die for the faith? One day, in a quiet time with God, I read through my church's doctrinal statement and the doctrinal statements of several Christian organizations and seminaries. I wanted to know what truths I would die for. I reasoned that if I knew what I would die for, I would know what to live for. Here are some truths I identified:

- *The inerrancy of Scripture.* My personal relationship with Jesus Christ is based upon the Bible. If the Bible is the basis for my relationship with him, I must be ready to defend it. God's Word is life. My heart would soon dry up without the precious nourishment from God's Word. I knew this was the first issue to live for—or die for.

- *The character of God.* God is Father, Son and Holy Spirit. He is the all-knowing, all-loving Creator and Sustainer of life. He is wholly good, righteous and unchanging. He is all-powerful and always faithful. God lacks nothing. He is utterly dependable.

- *The deity of Christ.* If Christ is not the eternal, incarnate God who died for the sins of human beings, then his sacrifice is not eternal and complete. If his sufficiency is limited, then my faith is in vain. Jesus *is* God, and his sacrifice *is* complete.

- *The Holy Spirit is God.* Jesus said another of the same kind would come to comfort, lead and guide us. God resides in me to live through me.

- *I am sinful.* My personal sinfulness separates me from the holy God. I am utterly imperfect; therefore, I need a mediator to reconnect my relationship. Christ is that mediator. Salvation is impossible through any other means.

- *God works through the church.* The church universal is God's method for reaching the world with his love. No, I won't die for a building, but I will die for the right to assemble, worship and proclaim the truth.

I also read through the U.S. Constitution, the Bill of Rights and Declaration of Independence. I would go to court for most of the words in those documents, but I would die for only a few of them. The right to govern ourselves in a democracy is important to me. I would also spend the rest of my life in a jail cell for the First Amendment, which guarantees freedom of religion and freedom of speech. For people to continue coming to Christ, the pen and the voice cannot be silenced. If necessary I would join my courageous sisters and brothers who spent years in concentration camps, behind communist walls or in the cells of hostile religious countries for the right to tell of Jesus. I would also go to jail, if necessary, for my right to bear and raise my own children, my right to be married, my right to vote and my right to live out my Christian convictions.

Then I asked myself *whom* I would be willing to die for. My husband, my children, friends, relatives . . . those I am discipling . . . the innocent and oppressed . . . the list grew.

Then I remembered the Scripture, "Rarely will anyone die for a righteous person—though perhaps for a good person someone might actually dare to die. But God proves his love for us in that while we still were sinners Christ died for us" (Rom 5:7-8 NRSV). Would I die for the unrighteous, the unholy, my enemies? My answer: *Yes, Lord. I am willing to risk my life if you give me the wisdom to know when to stand up for the oppressed and when to speak up to the oppressor.*

PASSION PURIFIED

In *A Man for All Seasons,* Sir Thomas More, faced with execution, is asked by the king and his court to recant his views of the king's divorce and remarriage. His family arrives and asks him to change his views. More replies, "When a man takes an oath . . . he's holding his own self in his hands. Like water. And if he opens his fingers, then he needn't hope to find himself again." To deny my convictions is to deny myself. Rejecting the passion God gives us will make life meaningless.

What so beats in your heart that if it were to vanish, you would no longer be you? Jeremiah said, "But if I say, 'I will not mention him or speak any more in his name,' his word is in my heart like a fire, a fire shut up in my bones. I am weary of holding it in; indeed, I cannot" (Jeremiah 20:9). Jeremiah was called to proclaim God's truth. Even if the people didn't respond—and they didn't—he still proclaimed because he was born to be a proclaimer!

What were you born to be? You can discover the passion that God designed *uniquely for you.*

Florence Nightingale was a selfless angel of mercy during the Crimean War and in the halls of London hospitals. In her journal she penned her passion for nursing: "O God, Thou puttest into my heart this great desire to devote myself to the sick and sorrowful. I offer it to Thee."

Florence fought for sanitation, good food and accurate records. In 1860 she founded the first school of modern nursing at St. Thomas's Hospital in London. It was not acceptable at that time for a woman to work so closely with the ill, but her passion propelled her past the stereotypes. After working and nursing the sick among peasant women, she wrote, "Now I know what it is to live and to love life. . . . I wish for no other earth, no other world than this."

Have you discovered what it means "to live and to love life"?

Have you discovered what it means "to live and to love life"? You have the opportunity to say with the prophet Habakkuk, "The Lord GOD is my strength, and He has made my feet like hinds' feet, and makes me walk on my high places" (Habakkuk 3:19 NASB). Passion will carry you to *your* high place. When you are there in the place of your passion, you can say, "I know who I was born to be."

LIVING IT OUT

As an experiment, write three sentences about times when you were moved to tears or action; or write four or five paragraphs of times you were other-centered and you felt that God used you. See if there is a common thread in the list. Any repeating words, people groups, common themes? God often repeats himself when he is trying to get our attention. Look for the repeating patterns to point the way to your passion.

Now interview one family member and two close friends. Ask them what topics you bring up most often. Are there any similarities between the lists you made and what the interviews reveal?

Finally, take your lists to the Lord. Also take a statement of faith from your church or a Christian organization. Ask God to show you what you are to live for. Commit the passion of your heart to God in prayer. Pray this simple but powerful prayer, "Lord, impassion my heart." Then watch and see what exciting opportunities God will unfold on your path.

INDIVIDUAL
Discovering Your Leadership Style

What you are is God's gift to you,
what you become is your gift to Him.

HENRIETTA MEARS

I love hats. One of the walls in my bedroom holds several hats that I've picked up at sales over the years. Recently a friend sent me an article about people who wear hats. A hat expert was quoted as saying that the only thing that doesn't go well with a hat is timidity. "You have to be more self-assured to wear a hat. . . . The moment you don't care what people think is the moment you've arrived." Women often comment to me, "Oh, I love your hats. I'd like to wear hats, but I don't look good in them." My usual reply is, "You just haven't found the right hat! Wearing a hat is an attitude you put on."

Carol Navratil, a courageous woman facing cancer, was given a "hat shower" by friends at a cancer rebound group. She was asked how she handled the transition from having hair to wearing hats. Her answer was her attitude. Donning a hat, she said, "Walk like it's supposed to be there."

Being a woman of influence is a matter of finding the right hat, then walking like it is supposed to be there! "For we are God's workmanship, created in Christ Jesus to do good works, which God prepared in advance for us to do" (Ephesians 2:10). He has promised to equip us for every good work; we just have to put on the hat!

ARE WE REALLY SO DIFFERENT?

Being a woman of influence is a matter of finding the right hat, then walking like it is supposed to be there!

When we put on the leadership hat, how do we lead? Studies show that men and women approach leadership differently. Sally Helgesen kept a diary that followed the lives of successful female executives and entrepreneurs. She found that women managers had many of the same characteristics as their male counterparts, but they also had a few distinctive character traits. She found that women managers

1. worked at a steady pace, as men did, but women guarded short "down times" to catch their breath and clear their mind throughout the day.

2. made a deliberate attempt to be accessible. One study showed that women managers were twice as accessible as their male counterparts.

3. integrated family and work. Men tended to compartmentalize their lives, while women blended them. It may be natural for a woman manager to make out her grocery list or talk to her children on the phone in the five minutes between meetings. How-

ever, men *and* women who carried a role conflict, being torn between family and work responsibilities, both wanted company policies that were more family-friendly, such as job sharing, flex time and child care.

4. preferred live personal contacts. Just like the male managers, females prefer conversations and delegation to be as personal as possible: they like face-to-face contact better than phone, memo or fax.

5. maintained a complex network of relationships outside the organization. Male managers spent equivalent time in outside contacts, but the women's networks were broader, often including volunteer organizations, ministry and personal interests that didn't seem as connected to the job.

6. focused on the ecology of leadership, which means women keep the long term in focus, while some male counterparts often felt buried in the "today."

7. saw their own identity as complex. A woman is not her career. Their careers were just one element of who women saw themselves to be.

8. scheduled time to share information. Women in leadership held relationships in high value. Women tended to see interruptions by people as an opportunity to share and build the relationship, not an interruption of a task.

Other studies on men and women on the job have noticed that women are slightly better at verbal skills, reading nonverbal clues, maintaining high energy and holding their own inner work standard. Men are slightly better at spatial tasks, attentiveness to power structures and task-oriented behaviors. Most important, men had a better ability to see themselves as leaders.

Differences between male and female leadership abilities can lead to complementary leadership styles, especially as women grow in self-confidence. When a woman has interacted with a group for an extended period and her leadership style is defined, others then see her competence. As she absorbs their responses to her, she then sees herself as a leader—and so does the group.

God plants within each of us desires, dreams, talents and skills to be used for his glory. Each of us has our own "hat" of responsibility to wear, and each is a different kind of leader. We can all uniquely influence the world around us.

On the next few pages you will find a leadership style test. I created this test after studying the roles of women in the Bible. It amazed me that women so different from each other could all be used by God in dramatic ways. This test can help you learn more about how God can use you as a woman of influence.

LEADERSHIP STYLE TEST

If a statement is *very true* about you, give it three points. If it is *sometimes true,* give it two points. If it is *rarely true,* give it one point. If you aren't sure, ask yourself, "Do I do this because I know it's right, or do I love doing it because it's who I am?" If it is out of obligation, give the statement a lower number. Remember, you are trying to discern the leadership style in which you will function best.

Leadership Style #1

___ I am drawn to detail work.

___ I notice those who need help (ill, hurting and so on), and I don't run away from needy people.

___ I like to create quietly.

___ I enjoy meeting the physical needs of others (food, water, medical care and so on).

____ I like having company in my home. I see myself as hospitable.

____ I want my material possessions to be used to help others, so I don't mind lending them out.

____ I like to nurture or encourage one-on-one, or even silently by doing nice things.

____ My friends see me as a mother at heart.

____ I don't mind serving. In fact, I don't like the spotlight, so I avoid drawing attention to something I've done.

____ Others compliment me on my ability to sacrifice.

____ **Total**

Leadership Style #2

____ I feel prayer accomplishes more than busywork.

____ I look forward to private worship and enjoy leading others in worship.

____ When someone asks me to pray, I make it a priority to remember to do it.

____ I like to use my talents as a way to worship God rather than just to meet people's needs.

____ I like to keep track of answers to prayer or prayer requests.

____ I understand the need for spiritual warfare, and I like to equip others in this area.

____ I like to be part of helping the tough-case people, such as drug addicts, gangs or the sexually deviant.

____ I don't enjoy the spotlight or crowds.

____ Others thank me for "being there" for them in tough times.

____ I like to counsel others when they are having problems.

____ **Total**

Leadership Style #3

___ Time gets away from me when I study the Bible. I enjoy long blocks of study time.

___ I like to prepare lesson plans. I can pick the main points out of what I read or hear.

___ I like to teach a consistent group of people.

___ I like to disciple younger believers.

___ I look for opportunities to share with others what I know, so they can know it too.

___ I prefer having a few close friends rather than many acquaintances.

___ I like to see pupils succeed, even if they pass me on the professional ladder.

___ I like to help clarify people's thinking.

___ Others thank me for teaching them how to do things.

___ I would rather manage people than products.

___ **Total**

Leadership Style #4

___ I like to speak in public.

___ I like meeting new people.

___ I like discussions, even if they get lively.

___ Hearing opposing opinions doesn't make me any less sure of my own. I'm not afraid of taking a public stand.

___ I regularly read the opinion page, listen to talk radio and watch TV news shows.

___ I love magazines and books because I can use things I've learned from them in conversation.

___ I like to persuade others.

____ I am drawn to sales or spokesperson positions.

____ I am comfortable talking about my personal religious beliefs in public.

____ Others compliment my verbal skills.

____ **Total**

Leadership Style #5

____ I was a cheerleader, or I wanted to be one, when I was younger.

____ Others see me as a visionary. I love to dream and plan.

____ I see the potential in people and circumstances.

____ I enjoy inspiring others and coaching them to their best.

____ I regularly write notes of encouragement or send cards for special occasions.

____ I have a long Christmas card list.

____ I am comfortable in social settings.

____ I like sentimental things like poetry, tear-jerker movies and photo albums.

____ I am an optimist.

____ Others thank me for believing in them.

____ **Total**

Add up your points for each leadership style. You will probably be strongest in one or two areas. If you have the same score in all areas, retake the test, asking yourself if this is really how you see yourself; or have someone who knows you well take the test as if they are answering for you.

The goal of the leadership test is not to pigeonhole you but to reveal the leader within. God designed you to influence your world; he wants you to see how you can accomplish this task while still being yourself. Now check the descriptions below to identify the various leadership styles.

LEADERSHIP STYLE #1: THE PROVIDER

"Render service with enthusiasm, as to the Lord and not to men and women" (Ephesians 6:7 NRSV).

The key trait of a *provider* is that she sees a need and quietly goes about the task of providing for the need. This woman leads from behind the scenes. She may be a gifted administrator. She may also have the gifts of helps, mercy, hospitality or giving. She won't call a press conference or rally the troops to get a need met. However, she is strategic at bringing together a small group of people to accomplish a task.

Providers see the details. They stick to the task until it is complete, and they stick to the person until the person is stable and self-sufficient. They are often commended for their loyalty. Providers lead from an open heart. They are drawn to professions where they can work quietly and consistently. It is in their faithfulness to the least of tasks that they gain their leadership platform. Providers keep computer systems up and running, staff hospitals, run hotels, make our food and keep organizations running. Providers are leaders like Martha, who took care of the physical needs of the Savior while he ministered. They may be behind the scenes making matzos, but their maturity runs deep. It was Martha who said, when her brother died, "Lord, . . . if you had been here, my brother would not have died. But I know that even now God will give you whatever you ask" (John 11:21-22).

The early church in Acts would not have gotten off the ground without the hostesses of the house churches. The temple would not have run without women like Anna, who served night and day making preparations. The personal touch would have been missing from the budding church without women like Tabitha and Lydia, who moved about quietly in their communities, providing for the needs of the less fortunate.

Providers often see their possessions as gifts from God and readily share their material goods to help others. One provider friend of mine has a special calling to encourage other women in ministry. She was raised in a ministry home, so she knows the unique stresses and pressures. She uses her gift of hospitality to refresh those on the front lines. A mother who is a provider always has extra snacks for the hordes of children who play at her house.

The only downfall of a provider is that she is so good at sacrificing for others' needs that she may judge others by their willingness or unwillingness to sacrifice. Children raised with a mother who parades her sacrifices can become bitter and guilty. But a mother who is truly sacrificial won't make herself a martyr, because she sees her sacrifice as just meeting the need of the moment.

Susannah Wesley had the heart of a provider. She studied Greek, Latin, French, logic and metaphysics—and she loved the Bible. She began a Bible study in her living room; it grew to a group of over two hundred. She used her knowledge as she single-handedly home-schooled her ten children. (She bore nineteen, but only ten survived past infancy.) Her mothering style was very deliberate. She taught her children from 9 a.m. until noon and listened to their recitations of verses from 2 to 5 p.m. daily. The discipline and self-control learned at their mother's knee launched two of her sons, Charles and John, into a dynamic work for God as they founded the Methodist movement.

Whether you are single or married, a mom or a grandmother, if you are a provider, a part of you really cares that things are done right. You want life to run smoothly and efficiently. People depend on you for your ability to make that happen. Your caring thoroughness will ensure your influence.

LEADERSHIP STYLE #2: THE PETITIONER

"This kind can come out only by prayer" (Mark 9:29).

The *petitioner* is an advocate. She represents the needs of others to God through prayer. She may be drawn into the field of law or social work. Or she may minister to gang members, prison inmates, addicts and others spiritually bound up by sin or circumstance. To a petitioner there are no tough neighborhoods. She has an outward fearlessness because she has an inward surety from God. She understands and communicates the need for spiritual warfare. She may be drawn to counseling because of her keen insight. People in need have a way of landing on her doorstep.

Deborah was a petitioner. God called Deborah to be a judge in a time in Israel's history when people were doing that which was right in their own eyes. She was spiritually in tune, and people knew it. She would sit under a tree and people would come from all around to have her judge their cases. But Deborah didn't just sit under the tree; she also got up and got involved. Barak, the general of the Israelite army, asked Deborah to go into battle with him—so Deborah went! And Israel won.

Mothers who are petitioners often have their children's friends come to them for advice. These mothers start prayer groups, organize neighborhood watches and float petitions. Mothers with this leadership style pray first and lecture little. One of my friends with this gift was asked by my son to pray for his "owie." When I asked him why he asked her instead of me, he said, "Mom, I know you can pray for me, but she prays all the time. I thought it would work quicker!"

Petitioner moms can be accused of overspiritualizing problems. One of my boys gets a little unruly if he is tired or hungry. Once a petitioner friend was amazed to see how quickly his negative mood became positive after he ate a sandwich. She confided to me that she had been praying for him because she thought he had a rebellious bent. I told her to keep praying because we all have a rebellious bent!

Elizabeth Dole has served under six presidents. In 1991 she became the first woman since Clara Barton to serve as president of the Red Cross. She is a bulldog fighting for good causes. Elizabeth grew into her leadership style under the examples of her grandmother and mother. Her grandmother lost a son when he was killed by a drunk driver. Every cent from the insurance policy went to build a mission hospital overseas. Elizabeth's most vivid memory of her mother is of her kneeling in prayer.

Elizabeth Dole looks for ways to give back to the community and make a difference. She loves giving reverse birthday parties, where guests bring donations for charity. Her first was a party at Sarah's Circle, a church-sponsored organization that houses the homeless in Washington, D.C. She says, "We can't take all God gives us, then do nothing for those less fortunate. The questions I'll want to ask myself when I'm ninety years old and looking back over my life are not, How much money did I make? and How many titles, awards, or honors did I receive? But rather, What did I stand for? Did I make a positive difference for others?"

LEADERSHIP STYLE #3: THE PREPARER

"All Scripture is God-breathed and is useful for teaching, rebuking, correcting and training in righteousness" (2 Timothy 3:16).

The woman is who is a *preparer* has the patience to teach and the conviction that teaching is important. The minute a preparer gains a skill, she wants to give it away by training someone else. She may be very accomplished in her field, but her real delight is training and equipping others. A preparer does not mind when her pupils pass her on the professional ladder; in fact she expects it and rejoices in it.

The preparer gets lost in studying. This woman loves the library, books, research, outlining and lesson prep. She often loses track of time when she is immersed in study.

The preparer loves to teach the same consistent group of students because growth in her students is her greatest reward. She doesn't mind speaking publicly, but she does it in order to equip others rather than because she can't keep quiet. Her method is her message. She wants others to have the "how-to's" of life.

Priscilla had the heart of a preparer. Along with her husband, she took Apollos aside to tutor him in theology because he had not received a complete education (Acts 18:24-28). Mentoring and discipling come naturally to preparers.

Mothers who are preparers have children who do household chores well at an early age. Preparers may love helping groups of children learn crafts or cooking. Kids love the homes of preparers because they come away feeling smarter.

However, preparer moms should also watch out for the "my way is the right way" mentality because it easily creeps into their teaching. If this happens, their children and those under their influence will feel defeated.

A. Wetherell Johnson, the founder of Bible Study Fellowship, had the heart of a preparer. Her method of small-group discussion accompanied by a lecture, take-home study notes and a lesson, has become a model for ministries throughout the world. Early in her ministry, she was asked to speak to a group of young people. She didn't want to merely give her testimony, so she decided to speak on a Scripture text. "I thought it would be easy," she wrote, "but I finished with embarrassment in less than five minutes, recognizing too late that speaking for God needed careful preparation." She went back and began preparing! And it is for her preparation skills that she is best known.

LEADERSHIP STYLE #4: THE PROCLAIMER

"I have not hesitated to proclaim to you the whole will of God" (Acts 20:27).

This woman *loves* to talk! She is comfortable meeting new people, and she has strong verbal skills. She loves to debate, negotiate, moderate and emcee events. She always has a story to tell. The *proclaimer* leads by being the spokesperson. She is not afraid to speak in public, and she's not afraid to take a public stand for her beliefs. She is tenacious when criticized and believes that the bad speech of others should be answered with more speech. She doesn't want her critics silenced, because she longs to persuade them to join her side.

The proclaimer gravitates to a career where she can earn a living by talking. She may be a salesperson, service representative, spokesperson, actor, talk-show host or media personality. Often you will find proclaimers in politics, serving as lobbyists or public relations specialists. In volunteer organizations, the proclaimer usually has the most contact with the public.

Beverly LaHaye has the heart of a proclaimer. During the 1970s she felt that women's concerns were being downplayed. In 1979 she gathered a group of women and formed Concerned Women for America. Today this group is the nation's largest public policy women's organization, with over 500,000 members nationwide.

Moms who are proclaimers are fun at the dinner table and at bedtime because they have great stories to tell. Their children often form opinions about serious issues at an early age. The children of proclaimers always know their parent's political affiliation. Proclaimer parents have to watch out for lecturing when they should be listening.

Huldah was a proclaimer who was summoned by King Josiah. Josiah found a scroll and wanted to know if it was of God. Huldah was probably a teacher, perhaps one who taught women from her home near the temple. Huldah confirmed that the scroll was of God. She also gave Josiah an encouraging prophecy regarding his future—and a harsh prophecy for rebellious Israel's future. Because of Huldah's brave proclamation, Josiah ordered the reading of the scroll before all of Israel. It is interesting that in the brief description of Huldah's proclamation, "This is what the LORD says" is recorded four times. Huldah obviously knew she was just a vessel, simply a voice for God (2 Kings 22:14-20; 2 Chronicles 34:22-28).

Sometimes people think proclaimers were born with a silver microphone in their hands, but often God raises proclaimers out of obscurity.

Amanda Smith was a scrubwoman born into slavery. Her first husband abandoned her, and the second died. As a Negro widow in the post-Civil War era, her options for employment were slim. Amanda had always loved God and been faithful to the church. Soon after her second husband's death, she felt a distinct call to preach. It was a very unlikely career decision. She traveled throughout the north and south, over to England and then to India.

Because of her gender, Amanda was sometimes seen as an agitator for the ordination of women or for women's voting rights. She replied, "The thought of ordination had never once entered my mind, for I had received my ordination from Him who said, 'Ye have not chosen Me but I have chosen you, and ordained you, that you might go and bring forth fruit.'"

LEADERSHIP STYLE #5: THE PRAISER

"Let us consider how we may spur one another on toward love and good deeds" (Hebrews 10:24).

The *praiser* is the woman who leads by encouragement. She cheerleads. She coaches others on her team toward success. This kind of leader is gifted with the ability to have great faith in God and believe him for the seemingly impossible. Others see her as a visionary because she can picture a bright future and strategize about ways to get there. Optimism is her most obvious quality.

The praiser is the woman who sees the potential in everyone. Because she is so good with people, she gathers friends as other women gather flowers. Her Christmas card list is a mile long, because staying in touch with people is important to her. She is not afraid of her emotions, and she allows herself to express emotional sentiments freely, especially if another person will be strengthened.

Children of praisers have great self-esteem! These women are the perpetual team moms. A praiser never misses an opportunity to applaud her child. Her children's friends love to play at the praiser's home, because it's always like a party and everyone leaves feeling good. However, her idealism can be a source of pain for the praiser and her family. Because the praiser is such an optimist, she can fall into the trap of overinflating her strengths or the strengths of her children. If they fail, it feels like a crushing blow.

Praisers are so optimistic that some people feel intimidated around them. For many people, the praiser's high goals and aspirations are so lofty that to do anything less is to fail. A true praiser sets high goals because they give God plenty of space in which to work. She sees any shortcoming as only a minor setback or a challenge to cause further growth. For the praiser, any movement at all is reason for excitement. Her goal is just to inspire others to try.

In the Bible, Miriam was a praiser. Exodus 14—15 gives the account of God parting the Red Sea to free Israel from Egyptian bondage. Miriam, seizing the moment, grabbed a tambourine and began to dance. Thousands of women probably poured out to join in the singing and dancing. Miriam sang God's praise: "Sing to the LORD, for he is highly exalted. The horse and its rider he has hurled into the sea" (Exodus 15:21). Israel needed to learn to praise again. Miriam, now well over eighty, cheered them into praise.

We all need to hear encouraging words to help us battle down our own negative thinking and the lies Satan throws our way. "I think that's why women with this leadership style are found in a broad range of professions. Every team needs a cheerleader; every person needs hope.

WHO IS YOUR AUDIENCE?

In ancient Israel, gifted handcrafters, artists and musicians were set apart for special work for the temple. In the same way, our leadership styles dictate the way in which we use the talents God gives us.

The audience we are seeking to reach can help us focus our leadership style and find the best use of our gifts. For example, some solo recording artists have a burden to sing to reach the unchurched, while others sing to inspire the church to action. Two different audiences, two different callings, but the same talent.

BREAKING THE STAINED-GLASS CEILING

The debate over women's role in church leadership has gone on for centuries, and it still continues. For a woman to be free to lead, she must answer her own questions about women in church leadership. Here are some thoughts from a few modern women leaders:

Anne Graham Lotz, daughter of renowned evangelist Billy Graham, explains her calling to teach the Word of God around the world by comparing her life to that of Mary Magdalene. Mary followed Jesus. She sat under his teaching. She followed him through his ordeal on the cross when all his disciples fled except John. She followed him as he was taken off the cross, and she helped prepare him for burial. She came early one morning bringing costly spices to his tomb. There Jesus revealed himself to her and told her to go and tell his disciples.

Just as Mary was commissioned, so Anne feels commissioned. "The authority is not in a position that I hold. The authority is in the Word of God and the power of the Holy Spirit that clothes it." The key is a servant's heart and an obedient attitude. "I am a woman under compulsion," Anne says. "I am locked in by the evidence to giving a verbal expression of what I know, what I've seen, what I've heard, what I've experienced by faith, what he [God] has said to me by his Word."

Jill Briscoe says, "The Holy Spirit decides what gifts you have. You do not decide." Our job as women of influence is to discover our gifts. Dr. Ruth Tucker says that the best argument for women in church leadership is that all of us, women as well as men, are required to obey the biblical commands to "Go and make disciples" (Matthew 28:19) and

God expects people of both genders to be obedient to his commands.

"Preach the Word; be prepared in season and out of season; correct, rebuke and encourage" (2 Timothy 4:2). God expects people of both genders to be obedient to his commands.

This question of a woman's role in Christian leadership will probably never be settled to everyone's satisfaction. We may never know all the answers, so the best course of action is to continue to ask questions even as we step out and influence. Gretchen Gaebelein Hull, in *Equal to Serve*, raises many thought-provoking questions that a woman of influence should seek to answer from the Bible so she can be true to God and herself:

• What advice does the Bible have for us on our quest for approval?

• Is our tradition scriptural?

• Will you give up your rights to yourself and any entitlement to a certain position—and obey his call?

• Will you accept the authority of God?

• In the end, whose approval really matters most to you?

A godly woman of influence will not circumvent the Bible in order to be the boss. She will embrace God's Word in order to find her unique place of leadership. As I have studied the issue of women's leadership in Scripture, I have found the following questions helpful:

- What is the context of this question or this passage of Scripture? Is this command specific for a particular day and time, or does this command cross cultures and time periods?

- What is the whole counsel of God on this issue? Where else in the Bible does the issue arise?

- What insights can I gain from the writings of Bible scholars and historians concerning this issue?

- What insights can I get from research into the original language?

PUT ON THE HAT!

Confidence in Christ is an attitude of dependence on him. "Not that we are competent in ourselves to claim anything for ourselves, but our competence comes from God" (2 Corinthians 3:5). We may not *feel* like wearing the hat of influence. We may not *feel* qualified. We may not *feel* committed. We may not *feel* motivated. But as we rely on God and act according to the gifts and abilities he gives us, our feelings will catch up. God will see to it that we have all the training and resources we need.

This poem helps me see influence through God's eyes.

"Where shall I work today, dear Lord?"
And my love flowed warm and free.
He answered and said, "See that little place?
Tend that place for Me."
I answered and said, "Oh no, not there!
No one would ever see
No matter how well my work was done,

Not that little place for me!"
His voice, when He spoke, was soft and kind.
He answered me tenderly,
"Little one, search that heart of thine,
Are you working for them . . . or Me?
Nazareth was a little place . . . so was Galilee."

Often big things grow out of obedience to small things. Fern Nichols was a mother and homemaker in Poway, California, when her two older boys entered public school. She asked God for a concerned friend who would pray with her, and Moms in Touch Ministry was born. Now there are approximately 20,000 groups in the United States, contacts in over 95 countries, and over 150,000 women involved in the ministry worldwide to pray an hour a week for their children and for their children's teachers and educational system. Fern Nichols humbly credits "just being available" as the reason God uses women like herself. "When we desire to abide in the vine daily, we never know what day he'll choose to change our life and the lives of others forever."

Being open to the unique leadership role God has for you will change your life—and the lives of others forever. Your influence is unique, so . . . grab your hat, and step into God's dream for you.

LIVING IT OUT

Ask a more mature woman who knows you fairly well to take the Leadership Style Test for you. Have her insert your name (instead of "I prefer to work behind the scenes," it will be "Pam prefers to work behind the scenes"), and see if her results are the same as yours. Talk about the similarities and differences.

3

INTIMATE
Connecting with Your Creator

You can't,

God never said you could.

God can,

He always said he would.

JILL BRISCOE

Oh no!" I screamed as I looked at the gas gauge in disbelief. It was one of those hectic, terrible, horrible, no good, very bad days. I had a to-do list the size of a city phone book, and now my car had sputtered to a halt on the freeway. It refused to move despite my pleadings: "We're almost to the off ramp, you can at least make it to there! Please move—just a little farther. Don't be out of gas. Not here. Not now!"

Out of gas. The phrase rang in my head. *That's how I feel, Lord. I've given and given so much lately. I'm running on empty.*

As I walked down the freeway toward the off ramp, I tried to rationalize. *God, you know I've been very busy—school, kids, work, minis-try, the house* . . . The words sounded hollow. I knew I had been ne-glecting my time with God and his Word. *You're right, Lord. This past week I have fed myself spiritually on about two minutes of devotional read-ing a day.* I thought about how physically drained I would become if I ate only one Twinkie a day. No wonder my spiritual tank was on the red *E,* just like my car.

CONNECTING WITH GOD

God invites us into a relationship of intimacy with him. The word "intimacy" comes from the Latin *intimus,* which means inner-most. God wants to let us in on his in-nermost thoughts. Partnering with the word *intimacy* is *enthusiasm,* which lit-erally means "God within." When we have God within us, and we place our-selves within God, the result is energy that is unstoppable because it is super-natural.

> *When we have God within us, and we place ourselves within God, the result is energy that is unstoppable because it is supernatural.*

We might think we have to wait until heaven to truly know God, but Jesus said, "This is eternal life: that they may know you, the only true God, and Jesus Christ, whom you have sent" (John 17:3). Eternal life begins the moment we are introduced to Jesus personally. The heart cry of the apostle Paul is captured in his words, "Whatever was to my profit I now consider loss for the sake of Christ. What is more, I consider everything a loss compared to the surpassing greatness of knowing Christ Jesus my Lord" (Philip-pians 3:7-8).

GETTING RECONNECTED

Some of us women have fallen prey to lies about ourselves and our relationship with God. One lie I heard over and over as a university student was that because I am a woman, I am alienated from the God of the Bible. The argument told me and every other woman that because God chose to reveal himself using the personal pronoun *he,* all *shes* are alienated from God.

Yes, God chose to reveal himself as *he;* but as we become connected to God, we find that God transcends the gender debate. God created both male and female in his image (Genesis 1:22). In Christ there is neither male or female (Galatians 3:28). God longs to be connected with each human individual, whether male or female. To be reconnected, all we have to do is ask. Just talk to God, as you would to a friend. Admit you are imperfect and you long to be accepted by him. Jesus came to earth to reconnect us to God; we need only receive the gift of his sacrifice on our behalf.

C. S. Lewis, the wonderful Oxford philosopher and writer, had one of his fictional characters explain that when people "are wholly His they will be more themselves than ever." God created us and he unleashes us to be all we can be.

God's Word, the Bible, is his love letter to you. Each woman can build her relationship with God by hearing, reading, studying, memorizing and obeying God's Word. Within its pages you will find everything you need for a life of hope and meaning. Kay Arthur, author of Precept Bible Studies, says, "Every child of God desperately needs a personal and intimate knowledge of the pure Word. . . . God gave us a lifetime and that's what it takes to mine the treasures of His Word."

Here are six simple methods I have found that every woman can use to study the Bible for herself:

1. *Be a news reporter.* In Journalism 101 we were taught a list of one-word questions to use in every interview: *Who? What? Where? When? Why? How?* You can open your Bible to any verse, ask these simple questions, write down the answers—and you will have learned the basics of that verse. *How* works best as an application question: "How can I use what I've just learned?"

2. *Be a psychologist.* Make yourself an observer of a person in the Bible. Read and record the person's words and actions. You can then draw out the person's character traits. The easiest way to accomplish a character study is to take a concordance, look up the person's name and record every verse that has anything to do with this character. Read the stories of the person in their context. Then answer these questions: What did _____ do? Who did _____ know? What did _____ say? What characteristic is described or implied? How can I become like _____? Why would I *not* want to become like _____?

3. *Be a florist.* Just as a florist gathers beautiful flowers from around the world to create a stunning bouquet, you can gather verses on a theme from throughout the Bible. Explore sticky questions such as "Why is there pain and suffering?" "How can I deal with my fears?" "What does God say about divorce?" Use your concordance to look up every word or phrase that could possibly be related to your question. For example, for a question about pain, I would look up *pain, suffering, persecution* and possible solutions such as *endure, long-suffering, steadfast* and so on. I would record the key thought of each passage. Then I would look for patterns, repeated words or ideas, commands and promises.

4. *Be a linguist.* When you read the Bible, you are reading a translation. The Old Testament was originally written in Hebrew, and the New Testament was originally written in Greek. Do word

studies to draw out deeper meanings. Hebrew is a language of pictures. Studying the word development of a Hebrew word will give you a visual aid opening up its meaning. Greek, on the other hand, is very exact. To find word meanings, I use *Strong's Exhaustive Concordance, The Theological Wordbook of the Old Testament* and *The Expository Dictionary of New Testament Words,* which have detailed instructions in their preface. I use good Bible commentaries to check the results of my studies.

5. **Be an English student.** If you take a Bible passage and put it into outline form, key features will pop out at you. First write out the verse(s) so the most important points are to the left and the lesser details fall to the right. Key words or phrases can be highlighted or boldfaced. For example, Colossians 1:10-12 could be written:

And we PRAY
   this in order that
      YOU MAY LIVE A LIFE WORTHY OF THE LORD
      and
      MAY PLEASE HIM
         in every way:
            bearing fruit
            in every good work,
            growing
               in the knowledge of God,
            being strengthened with all power
               according to HIS glorious might
          so that you may have
            great endurance
              and
            patience,
              and

> joyfully giving thanks
> to the Father,
> who has qualified you to share
> in the inheritance
> of the saints
> in the kingdom of light.

From writing the verse in outline form, I can clearly see several key issues to commit to prayer. I might want to study the key points first so I can be more specific in my application. My study outline might look like this:

MY PRAYER FOR A WORTHY WALK

I. What pleases God

A. Bearing fruit

B. Growing in the knowledge of God

C. Being strengthened with all power

II. Results of pleasing God

A. Great endurance

B. Patience

C. Joyfully giving thanks

1. Because God is my Father

2. Because God qualified me to share in inheritance

This outline could serve as my quiet time outline for an entire week. I could do theme and word studies to try to figure out just what Paul was praying for the believers in Colossae. I could then apply these to prayers for myself and the ones I seek to influence.

6. *Be an artist.* In Molly Newman and Barbara Damashek's play *Quilters,* one character says as she stitches, "Each block is different. Each pattern has a thread of somebody's life running through

it. You'll see my thread in there from time to time with all the others . . . my memories, my hopes, my dreams, my prayers."

One artistic friend of mine struggled with her daily quiet time. She felt pressured to make her journal perfect. She lamented that she didn't get the "right" answers when she used more intellectual study methods. She found herself dreading her time with God rather than looking forward to it. She said, "I want to grow in my knowledge of God. And I really want to know God's Word. But all the methods I've tried make me feel distant from him."

I suggested, "Treat your quiet time journal like a sketchpad. Each day write down a special verse or just a word or two that you find meaningful. Marking up your Bible creatively might help you visually understand a passage better. You could mark promises with rainbows. In my Bible I mark special verses with hearts and asterisks. You can use a variety of symbols to decorate a passage and get a grasp of key ideas. In your journal, write down how it touched you or applies to you. Then depict it in an artistic way. God made you an artist, so he'll speak to your artistic heart."

Donna, a woman who designs beautiful hand-stitched quilts, studied Genesis for a year in a small group Bible study. Inspired by God's creative work, she stitched a quilt depicting the seven days of creation. The Word of God had gone in through her head, down through her heart and out through her hands.

A PERSONAL CONNECTION

I feel connected to God by my confidence that he is personal and knowable. Jesus wept over Jerusalem and longed to gather her people as a mother hen gathers her chicks under her wings (Luke 19:41; 13:34). God promises, "I know the plans I have for you . . . plans to prosper you and not to harm you, plans to give you hope and a future" (Jeremiah 29:11). God reveals himself as a personal being—not a force, not a philosophy, not even a religion. God's arms are always open, wanting to embrace me; the choice is mine whether to flee from or run to that embrace.

A strong connection with God can carry us through unthinkable circumstances. Gracia Burnham is the widow of Martin Burnham, who served for seventeen years as a missionary pilot in the Philippines. A radical terrorist group kidnapped the Burnhams and held them hostage in the jungle for more than a year. The U.S. military tried a surprise attack to free them. Martin was caught in the crossfire and died. Gracia explained how she made it through that year and since. "God says He doesn't test you beyond what you are able to endure. I think each person's testing must be in proportion to what faith God has given them. I don't think I was able to drum up any special faith when I was going through this. I think it was all God's doing. He gave me what I needed day by day. Walking closely with Him and knowing His Word well is really going to help you when you face whatever testing comes your way."

Another missionary, Nancy Mankin, understands the strength of connection with God. Nancy and her husband, Dave, were reclining in their hammocks and enjoying an evening of quiet conversation on their missionary base in Panama. Suddenly three men rushed in and pointed automatic rifles at them. One of the men told Nancy to say her goodbyes. She leaned toward Dave and said, "I'm going to kiss you goodbye."

Dave answered, "Do you think they'll let you?"

Nancy calmly replied, "They said, 'Say your goodbyes.'" Then the two kissed and Dave was marched out into the night.

Even though she was in the worst possible moment of her life, God gave Nancy the strength and wisdom to make quick decisions which helped save the lives of everyone else in the camp. Just two weeks earlier, she had asked Dave to explain what to do if guerrillas came and took the men and left the women. Dave thought the question odd; he thought probably all would be taken or all would be killed. But Nancy persisted, and Dave explained a plan of escape downriver. It was that plan that carried the women and children to safety.

Nancy credits God with her ability to maintain a cool head in such horrific circumstances. She also credits God with the supernatural peace that comes through a personal connection with God. In a very private and individual way, God has enabled her to keep going on, day after day, as she and the other family members awaited for years news of the fate of their men. Nancy clung to a quote from Hannah Whitall Smith's *Safe Within Your Love:*

> I feel just like a little chick who has run out of a storm and under his mother's wings and is safe there. I hear the raging of the storm and I am utterly unable to comprehend it or measure the damage it is doing. But I am safe under His wings. He can manage the dark storm but I cannot. Why then should I worry or be anxious? . . . When I feel hopeless or fear, I know I need to get back under His Wings.

Nancy's husband was among those killed by the guerrilla soldiers. Today Nancy continues to tuck herself under God's wing, which is the safest place to be.

AN EMOTIONAL CONNECTION

When I was pregnant with my third son, one of my best friends, Tamera, was also pregnant. After church one Sunday, Tamera sensed I needed a break. We packed up both of our families and headed to a park for a picnic. Our conversation turned to how we handle adversity. "You always just go on," Tamera said with a smile. She didn't need to say any more. She had already shared with me the major and minor trials that had accompanied the births of each of her three sons. Tamera was now expecting a baby girl.

A few weeks later, late at night, I got a call from Tamera's husband. Their baby girl had been born, but the doctors had told them that she would not live long. The next few days I walked through this valley with my friend. Sooner than I was ready for it, I got the call: "She's home with Jesus. I rocked my baby into Jesus' arms."

Tamera wept. I wept. Jesus wept. Often we forget that Jesus too felt deeply—*feels* deeply. When his dear friend Lazarus died, Jesus knew the pain of Lazarus's sisters Mary and Martha. Each told him, "Lord, if you had been here, my brother would not have died." When Jesus saw the grief of the sisters and those with them, "he was deeply moved in spirit and troubled" (John 11:32-33). By the tomb, Jesus himself wept. He knew he was going to raise Lazarus from the dead, yet he was still moved. God incarnate was emotionally connected to his people's pain.

By Tamera's side through the days of funeral preparation and the memorial service I saw God emotionally connect with her in a way I could not. When I brought food after the funeral, I found this note on her door: "Shall we accept good from God, and not trouble?" (Job 2:10).

Borrow a friend's faith if you have to, but hang on to Jesus.

Some days Tamera's grief would overwhelm her and she would say, "Pam, I want to believe this will be turned into good."

"I do too. I'll loan you my faith to believe," I offered.

"I'll take it! I want to hang on . . . to life . . . to God . . . to hope." She didn't know why this had happened or how she was going to go on with life, but she tenaciously held on to God.

Borrow a friend's faith if you have to, but hang on to Jesus. Tamera kept the connection open with God. Just about one year after her precious daughter's death, new life again came into her arms. Tamera delivered a healthy baby girl!

Carol Kent, a popular Christian speaker, took a walk one day with her beloved husband, Gene, and they talked about how great life was. Their ministry Speak Up with Confidence had taught thousands to communicate their faith. Their son, a highly decorated officer and a graduate of the Naval Academy, was married and they had two precious new granddaughters.

Then the unthinkable happened. They received a call that their only son was in jail, charged with murder! In her book *When I Lay My Isaac Down*, Carol writes of a key decision she made early in her ordeal of pain:

> In a deeply personal way we realized that when the unthinkable circumstances enter your life, there comes a point when you either stand by what you believe or you walk away from it. Over time, we chose the powerful reaffirmation of our foundational posture in the universe: God was God and we were not. We were utterly dependent upon Him, and if we were to continue living with a sense of purpose and passion, we knew our only hope was in His infinite mercy and his unshakable plan for redemption regardless of sin, sorrow and shame.

Carol and God have navigated down a path she never imagined. The greater the pain, the further she dug into the Word of God. One day as we sat next to each other on a panel for military wives whose husbands were deployed, she revealed the source of her strength. She said at first she struggled to continue speaking. Then through wise counsel, she began to embrace the fact that Satan was waging an all-out attempt to silence her voice, and that of her godly extended family, as a megaphone for the gospel. She went from wanting to avoid the pulpit to "feeling like I was stepping on Satan's head each time I began to teach." Satan tried to silence the message of God, but instead God turned up the volume. Carol's voice has gotten louder and stronger as she has forged an even more powerful and intimate connection with her Creator.

AN ATTENTIVE CONNECTION

God wants to hear about our cares, not because he needs to hear but because we need to tell him. A preschooler accidentally spilled his fruit punch on the floor. He decided to clean up the mess himself and dashed to the back porch to get the mop. Suddenly realizing it was dark outside, he became apprehensive about reaching out the door for the mop. His mother reminded him that Jesus was everywhere—even in the dark. The boy thought for a minute. Then, putting his face to the door he said, "Jesus, if you are out there, will you hand me the mop?"

Sometimes when you pray, your mind may wander. Don't heap guilt on yourself. Simply pray through the area that has come into your mind. God wants to address that area of

Prayer doesn't change God; it changes me.

your life. Perhaps Satan is tempting you in that area, and God wants to get your attention. Or it may be an area of selfishness from which God wants to free you.

The movie *Shadowlands* is the love story of C. S. Lewis and Joy Davidman Gresham. Lewis married late in life, and soon afterward Joy was diagnosed with cancer. Lewis prayed and prayed as her health deteriorated. In the movie a theological colleague comments that surely all of Lewis's prayers had changed the plan of God. Lewis replies, "I pray because the need flows out of me all the time . . . it [prayer] doesn't change God, it changes me."

A connection with God changes how we make decisions and gives us a supernatural source of wisdom. One of my mothering role models calls her family together to fast and pray if one of her children is experiencing extra stress or facing a big decision. Every one of her four children has a strong relationship with Jesus. All have spent part of their adult lives in full-time ministry and are now using their careers to further God's kingdom in the world.

Before every big decision, I take an extended time away to spend with God. Before Bill and I married, before Bill went back to school, before we decided on seminary, before we had each of our three boys, before we left youth ministry, before we accepted a pastorate, before we built a house, before I returned to school, before every book, we always set aside a day to pray.

Bill and I set aside special days to pray before major transitions in our boys' lives such as starting school or entering puberty. Each August, before the boys begin school, we set aside one day as our "Learner and Leader" day. We do something fun as a family; then, over a meal, we negotiate privileges and responsibilities for the next year. Bill and I also choose a special gift for each son that will encourage the leadership trait he will be working on for the next year. We give each son his gift along with a verbal blessing, and then we pray for him. (A complete picture of our parenting choices is in our book, *10 Best Decisions a Parent Can Make*.)

A Unique Connection

To keep my relationship with Christ fresh, I use regular mornings or afternoons away, which I call my "dates with Jesus." I take along my Bible, my prayer notebook, my journal and a concordance. I may also take a book on a particular topic, an informative or inspiring article, my daily planner and a devotional book. I usually have a topic that I want to research or a decision for which I need to spend time in the Word. I deal with distractions by writing them out in a journal and finding verses that apply. I have my own personal worship service with singing and extended prayer. Each time is different, but each time I am renewed.

We don't have to get away for an extended period to focus on God. I look for quiet moments throughout my day to refocus my heart. Right before I rise and before I doze off at night, in the shower and as I blow-dry my hair, or any other time can be time for a "holy huddle" with God. I love to swim laps and take walks because I can shut away the outside world and focus on God. I can even make a cramped airline seat a holy oasis as I flip open a Bible and turn on a praise chorus on the iPod.

Bible memorization helps my prayer connection. After twenty-four hours we may accurately remember 5 percent of what we hear, 15 percent of what we read, 35 percent of what we study, 57 percent of what we see and hear, but 100 percent of what we memorize.

When I marinate chicken, it is still 100 percent chicken, but it no longer smells or tastes the same. As we "marinate" ourselves in the Word, we are still ourselves, but with the savory flavor of one who has been in God's presence.

A woman of influence is wise to protect her quiet connections with God. Each woman will find her own intimacy rhythm. The goal is intimacy, not legalistic ritual.

A friend with small children told me that she felt guilty because she didn't get up an hour before her family and spend time with God. She was functioning on less than five hours of sleep, and she found it impossible to carve out the time during the day. I asked her, "Why does the time have to be in a single one-hour block?"

I explained that often I prefer to spread out my intimate moments with the Lord. "First thing in the morning, I read a small section of Scripture. I claim a phrase or a verse as mine for the day. On my mirror are verses I am working on memorizing. I repeat them as I blow-dry my hair and put on my makeup. Over lunch, I like to do my Bible study. In the car, I listen to praise music and I pray. In the evening, after the kids are in bed, I journal my thoughts and note any specific requests or answers to prayer in my prayer notebook. At the end of the day my heart is drawn to Christ in worship, because I feel I have been in his presence all day."

God knows your life and will meet you there. At a conference, I heard Ruth and Billy Graham's daughter Anne Graham Lotz describe her mother's quiet time rhythm. Ruth was handling the raising of the children while Billy traveled doing revivals. Leisurely devotional times were hard for her to find. Ruth placed her Bible on the kitchen counter, and each time she walked by she read and meditated on a new phrase or verse. Anne explained that the Word of God "walked" into her mother's heart and life.

Communing with Jesus is not something you do; it is a place where you dwell. Intimacy means being with Jesus.

Communing with Jesus is not something you do; it is a place where you dwell. Intimacy means being with Jesus. I am open to changing any pattern of prayer or Bible reading, because I am open to Jesus changing me.

A NURTURING CONNECTION

As God nurtures us, we can encourage others in their relationship with God. Teresa Muller is a dear friend who is also a songwriter and recording artist. One of her songs ministered to me long before God brought her into my life.

Teresa was coming home from visiting her mother in the hospital. Her heart was heavy, and she talked to God about her feelings. As she prayed, a melody came clearly into her mind. She began to weave her feelings and the melody together into a song:

You are the Rock of my salvation,
You are the strength of my life,

You are my hope and my inspiration,
Lord, unto you do I cry.
I believe in you, believe in you,
For your faithful love to me.
You have been my help in time of need.
Lord, unto you do I cleave.

"You Are the Rock of My Salvation" was a song I sang through depression after a move. It was a song I sang as I prayed all night for my friend Tamera in her crisis. "You Are the Rock of My Salvation" has encouraged me before speaking engagements, during exams and throughout personal trials. I can't read music, but my heart can sing because a woman of influence like Teresa opened up her relationship with Jesus and let me in.

JUST A TOUCH

One woman was desperate for a connection to God. She was very ill with a menstrual disorder. She was weak from the blood loss and even weaker from the doctors' mistreatment. She also felt desperately lonely. Her condition made her an outcast in her society. Everyone thought she had somehow brought her problems on herself.

One day the woman's desperation drove her over the line of social and religious customs. She was going to get help for her problem, and she was going to do whatever it took. She'd heard about a man who had solutions to every kind of problem. And that man was only a few feet away from her. She thought, *If I can only touch the hem of his garment, I will be well.* She pushed her way through the crowd. Her frail hand reached through the throng gathered around him and— just a touch—her finger reached the edge of his cloak. At that moment, the bleeding stopped.

The swarming crowd carried the man out of her grasp. But Jesus turned and asked, "Who touched me?"

His disciples were outraged at the question. How were they supposed to know? After all, this was a crowd pressing in from every side.

Timidly the woman fell at Jesus' feet and said, "It was I." Jesus answered, "Daughter, your faith has healed you" (Mark 5:34). His power healed her infirmity, but his personal words to her healed her heart. For in that instant, all the crowd knew she was now clean and invited back into society.

Just a touch will keep you connected; a touch will give you the power to live above life's circumstances. A touch—a connection with God—will influence your heart and then in turn influence others. How's your connection? Reach out today. Catch a fresh hold on Christ's garment of love for you.

LIVING IT OUT

Choose at least one new intimacy idea from the following list to try out each day this week.

1. Make your prayers more concrete by writing them out as a letter to Jesus.

2. Go on a prayer walk, talking to the Lord as you walk along.

3. Pray through Scripture. Write out verses and personalize them with your name. For example, Psalm 84:11 (NASB): "No good thing does He withhold from Pam who walks uprightly."

4. Make a poster of a favorite verse. You may want to take a photo and have it developed as a poster, then write the verse on the poster.

5. Mark verses in a Bible that you think will help a particular child in the transitions to come. As you read, try to picture God through the child's eyes. Give the Bible to the child as a gift.

6. Make "devotion baskets" and place them in several areas of your

home. Decorate each basket and place in it a pen, a Bible, a devotional or inspirational book, and paper.

7. Sing during your entire time with God. You may want to try your hand at songwriting too.

8. Dance before the Lord like David (2 Samuel 6:14-15). Maybe you enjoy Jewish dancing or ballet. Dedicate your dancing to Christ.

9. Begin a miracle scrapbook. Keep photos and mementos that remind you of God's grace to you.

10. Write down every sin that continues to haunt you. Then write out 1 John 1:9 over the list as a statement of God's forgiveness. Destroy the list; God has already done so.

11. Write out a Philippians 4:8 list. What is lovely to you, worthy of praise, excellent and so on?

12. Pray in a manner you are not accustomed to. Try on your knees, or prone, or standing with your face to the heavens and your hands raised in worship.

13. Prepare a way to speak out for Jesus. Write a letter or create a greeting card. Write to a newspaper or create an ad campaign.

14. Give a gift to God. Donate anonymously to someone in need.

15. Go to a Christian bookstore and try out a new Bible study resource, the Bible on CD or Scripture set to music.

16. Praise Jesus from A to Z. "Jesus, you are amazing, beautiful . . ."

17. Try repeating every verse you have memorized, in order, from Genesis to Revelation. Stop at the first book you don't have a verse from, and learn one.

18. Make a promise notebook. List areas of hurt or need in your life. As you come to a verse that shows how God can meet the need, write it down. You're creating your own book of promises.

19. Read your favorite hymn. Find the Scripture on which it was based. Try to find out the story behind how the hymn was written.

20. Reread your sermon notes from last Sunday, or read ahead on the passage to be covered this Sunday.

21. Think back and picture your life before you were a Christian. What has Jesus "saved" you from?

22. Over each chapter number in your Bible, write your own subtitle. Use a different version of the Bible from time to time.

23. Fast from food, TV or a hobby in order to spend a longer time with God.

24. Write about your relationship with God from a different point of view. For example, my teenage son might say about me, "Mom—she has a radical walk with Jesus. She gets so stoked (excited). Awesome, dude."

25. Memorize a prayer from the Bible. Mary's prayer in Luke 1:46-55 is a good start.

26. Write and thank people who helped you grow in your walk with God this year. Or write to mentors from the past.

27. Write out a list of theological questions you'd like answered. Choose one and start researching it.

28. Go to church early. Walk the rows, sit in different places and pray for others who will sit there later.

29. Exercise to Christian music.

30. Tell one person who doesn't know Christ that you do know and love him.

Commit to spending at *least* five minutes a day with Jesus. If you need help getting going, check out the *One Year Book of Devotions for Women on the Go,* which I coauthored with Stephen Arterburn.

4

IDEALISTIC
Daring to Dream

You pay God a compliment by asking great things of Him.

TERESA OF ÁVILA

A woman in a big hat stood before the crowd. She was single, and she was single-minded. "It is the individual who counts. One man, Luther, started the Reformation in Germany. One man, Moses, led the children of Israel out of Egypt. One man, Paul, carried the gospel to the Roman empire. God always works through the individual." Henrietta Mears's idealism has affected the church as much as anyone of her time.

Henrietta Mears was a schoolteacher from the Midwest who landed at Hollywood Presbyterian Church in 1928. She ran the Sunday school department and turned it into a huge success. She also saw a need for high-quality, grade-appropriate material, so she and a friend wrote what they needed. Their curriculum became the core of Gospel Light Publishing. She saw a need to train young people, so her college department swelled and hundreds of lives were changed. She believed that camping provided a wonderful atmosphere for students to do some serious reflecting, so she founded Forest Home Conference Center, one the United States' most respected camping facilities.

Henrietta Mears challenged individuals to influence. One night after a college-age group's sharing time, she stood to her feet and said,

> This is the most ridiculous testimony time I think I have ever heard! All we have been talking about is silly little things that don't amount to a hill of beans. Have we lost sight of why we are here?
>
> There hasn't been one word about winning the nations for Christ. How about these great campuses in this area? Hasn't anything been done out at UCLA this week? Hasn't anyone witnessed to a student at USC?
>
> God weeps over these lost students, and we come here to talk about trifles. St. Paul dreamed about kingdoms brought to Christ. Knox cried, "Give me Scotland or I die." Luther wept over Germany.

After World War II, Henrietta gathered former students, now leaders, for a recommissioning and vision-setting gathering. The group represented over fifty Christian organizations. Attendees included Richard Halverson, who went on to be chaplain of the U.S. Senate; Louis Evans Jr., who went on to pastor several growing churches, including one in Washington, D.C.; and Bill Bright, who just a few years later started Campus Crusade for Christ.

DREAMING THE IMPOSSIBLE

Henrietta Mears was only one woman, but she had a big dream. Once she said, "There is no magic in small plans. When I consider my ministry, I think of the world. Anything less than that would not be worthy of Christ nor of his will for my life."

There is no magic in small plans.

Some days I wonder if I have a great plan—or *any* plan. If you can't figure out how socks disappear in the washing machine or where you put your car keys, is it possible to be part of God's great plan for using your life to change the *world?* Have no fear—it is possible!

Idealists envision life as it can be rather than as it is. Idealists are sometimes criticized as so heavenly minded that they are no earthly good. In *Man of La Mancha,* Don Quixote is treated as a fool and madman because he dares to dream the impossible dream. But without those who dream the impossible, we would all live in a much grimmer world.

Without idealists, many of us would still be riding in the back of the bus, many would have no voice at the polls, many would still be in chains and rags and treated as less than human. Without idealists, no woman would be educated or allowed to vote or own a business or property or hold political office. Idealists make the world a better place, not because all their dreams are fulfilled but because with each dream one step of progress is taken, one more need is fulfilled, one more glimpse of hope is given.

Christian idealists have their hopes rooted in the person of God. The clearer your vision of God, the clearer your vision of life and your own possibilities.

A LETTER FROM THE LORD

For years, each time I would hit a tough circumstance or feel depressed, I would search for a Scripture verse to encourage me. Soon several pages in my Bible became dog-eared. Then I hit a very lonely time after a move to a new city. I called a friend, Mary, and in the course of our conversation she shared a principle she had just heard at a leadership conference. Mary asked me, "What attribute of God are you not believing?"

I knew that I needed to get a fresh view of the God whom I said I loved and who I thought loved me. I strung together the verses from the dog-eared Bible pages and personalized them in the form of a letter from God to me. Since that time, these verses have encouraged me to step out, try the improbable and believe God for the impossible. The letter now hangs in my home to remind me daily of who God is and of his personal love for me. Here is my letter:

What attribute of God are you not believing?

Dear Pam,

Nothing is impossible for Me. I am able to do immeasurably more than all you can ask or think. In Me all things were created, in heaven and on earth, visible and invisible . . . thrones . . . powers . . . rulers . . . authorities. All things were created by Me, and I am before all things, and in Me all things hold together.

Mine is the greatness and the power and the glory and the majesty and the splendor. . . . I am exalted as head over all. Wealth and honor come from Me. In my hands are strength and power to exalt. . . . Nothing on earth is my equal!

It is not by [your] might nor by [your] power but by my spirit. . . . I know when you sit down and when you rise; I perceive your thoughts from afar. . . . I am familiar with all your ways. Before a word is on your tongue I know it completely. . . . You cannot flee from my presence. If you go up to the heavens, I am there; if you make your bed in the depths, I am there. If you rise on the wings of the dawn, if you settle on the far side of the sea, even there my hand will guide you, my right hand will hold you fast. . . . Even the darkness is as light to Me.

I stretch out the heavens like a canopy and spread them out like a tent to dwell in. . . . I measure the waters of the earth in the hollow of my hand, and with the breadth of my hand I mark off the heavens.

I am the Creator. I am the Wonderful Counselor, the Mighty God, the Everlasting Father, the Prince of Peace. I am the Alpha and Omega . . . the Beginning and the End.

I am immortal and dwell in unapproachable light . . . [yet I tell you:] Approach my throne of grace with confidence, so that you may receive mercy and find grace to help in time of need.

I do not grow tired or weary; I have understanding no one can fathom. . . . My judgments are unsearchable, my paths . . . beyond tracing out! My thoughts are precious and vast are the sum of them! No one fully understands my mind. . . . No one instructed Me. No one taught Me the right way. . . . No one can compare . . .

I hem you in before and behind. . . . Be convinced that neither death nor life, neither angels nor demons, neither the present nor the future nor any powers, neither height nor depth nor anything else in all creation can separate you from my love.

To this day, when I hit a tough place, I will look up verses by topic, string them together and pray them over my life or the situation. If I am fearful, I string together verses on courage; if weary, verses on God's strength; if wondering what path to take, verses on God's anointing, favor or wisdom. A concordance or a resource such as Biblegateway.com will help with this exercise.

Praying God's Word reminds me of who God is. The Word of God is sharper than a double-edged sword (Hebrews 4:12), and the truth will set us free (John 8:32). The power is not in me but in the truth of the Word and the power of the promise-making, prayer-answering God.

WORD PICTURES OF GOD

God reveals much about himself through the names he calls himself in Scripture. If we can carry these pictures of God around with us, we can accomplish much more of what we dream. For example, one of my favorite names of God is *Jehovah-raah,* "The Lord is my shepherd."

I grew up on a Suffolk sheep farm in eastern Idaho. Year after year, we would watch the tiny lambs being born. Inevitably some lambs were rejected or orphaned and needed tender loving care to survive. My brother, my sister and I would each get to choose a 4-H lamb from these "bummer" lambs.

At age ten, my first year in 4-H, I had a little lamb that I named Bunny because he loved to hop from rock to rock like a rabbit. For eight months Bunny and I went everywhere together. I'd hold Bunny. I'd card his soft, lanolin-coated wool. I'd feed and water him. I'd practice showing him. It was pretty much "everywhere that Pammy went, the lamb was sure to go."

Bunny and I did well at the county fair. But then came auction day. As I knelt in the noisy ring, I couldn't fully comprehend what was taking place. I heard the gavel slam down and the auctioneer announce, "Sold!" A man motioned for Bunny and me to go down a chute. Then someone yelled to me, "Let him go!"

I started to cry. I thought, *I am the worst Bo-Peep ever!*

About eight years later, I sat in a quiet dorm room and read Jesus' words: "My sheep listen to my voice; I know them, and they follow me. I give them eternal life, and they shall never perish; no one can snatch them out of my hand" (John 10:27-28). My eyes welled up. I realized I would never suffer the fate of my lamb Bunny. I was God's lamb, and no one could snatch me out of his hand. I would never be separated from his care. Knowing I'm secure in the Good Shepherd's care gives me courage even when things get rough and I can't see any purpose for what is happening.

HIS NAME IS WONDERFUL

Whenever I feel weak or vulnerable, I go to the Psalms. There the poet's pen quenches my fears with beautiful word pictures of the person of God. My idealism returns as I read how God surrounds me like a shield, that he is my rock, my fortress, my stronghold, my bulwark. Being the mother of three boys, I have firsthand experience with such portraits of war.

One summer the boys and I studied swords, shields and other defenses against enemy attacks. We wanted to re-create some of these instruments of defense to play away a long, hot afternoon. But as we studied, I realized my impressions of these items were based more on cartoons than on the Bible!

When God says he is our *shield,* he doesn't mean some tiny tin plate with a fancy crest. A shield in David's time was heavy; it wrapped around three sides of a person and was big enough for a large warrior to hide behind. The only ways to get hurt in battle were to come out from behind the shield or to run away in retreat and get hit from behind! Everything that this fallen world may send my way has to go through the character of God and his loving plan for me first. That's my kind of shield!

The *rock* means a solid place, high enough to give perspective. It was usually there that the stronghold or fortress was built. Cities in the Old Testament were self-sufficient, so that when attack came, the walls would enclose the inhabitants in safety and they would have food and water. When I am resting in God and his character to fight my battles, I have everything I need to survive.

Finally, when the enemy of my life rails against me, I need to run into my *bulwark.* A fortress often had tall, usually circular, towers at its corners. In the towers were small slits, each just large enough to shoot an arrow out through it. From this vantage point, archers could clearly see the enemy approaching, yet they were protected from harm while they prepared their response to the attack. God is the only safe place I can run to, in order to gain the wisdom and insight to form a battle plan for my life.

Not only are we outwardly protected by God; we are protected by his indwelling Holy Spirit. The Spirit in our hearts is our pledge from God (2 Corinthians 1:22 NASB). The word *pledge* is the same word used for a deposit or down payment. It was also used to describe an engagement ring. God made a down payment of love by giving us the indwelling Holy Spirit.

When I am resting in God and his character to fight my battles, I have everything I need to survive.

God by his very character is able to be all we need. Mary Slessor knew God that way. As a young woman she paddled her canoe into the jungles of Calabar (now Nigeria). She was headed further inland to a tribe of cannibals. She had already spent years working against both tribal superstition and the exploitation of white traders. The traders had introduced rum and guns but had brought the African people no light, no hope, no help. As she paddled, Mary wondered, *Who am I, a weak woman, to face wild savages alone?* But she knew God. In *Our Faithful God: Answers to Prayer* she wrote, "My life is one long daily, hourly, record of answered prayer. For physical health, for . . . guidance given marvelously, for errors and dangers averted, for enmity to the gospel subdued, for food provided at the exact hour needed, for everything that goes to make up life and my poor service, I can testify with full and often wonder-stricken awe that I believe God answers prayer."

Mary Slessor's relationship with God helped her battle superstitious practices. The most brutal was the custom of throwing newborn twins to the wild animals because of the belief that twins were a curse. She took these children into her home and raised them as

"God and one are always a majority."

her own, and through the years she took in many more children besides.

At age sixty-seven, Mary Slessor finally succumbed to the malaria that had plagued her throughout her thirty-eight years in Calabar. She was surrounded by a large crowd of Christian men and women, her now grown adopted children and children of their own. Tribespeople in Calabar mourned the loss of the woman who wrote in the margin of her Bible: "God and one are always a majority."

WHO ARE YOU, DAD?

Nothing in your self-concept or your past is too big to keep you from reaching the goals God has for you. As we see God as he is, we will be able to see ourselves as he sees us, as women of influence. We are chosen, gifted, accepted by our Father. God can help us overcome the past and even use it to propel us and those we love into a more positive place.

My father has struggled with alcoholism most of his life. He is a goodhearted man who has been wounded and carries a lot of emotional baggage. He has sought to drown the pain with a bottle. However, alcohol not only drowns the pain—it drowns the person. My dad's good heart and gentle nature became bitter and calloused. The man who desired to always be there for his kids, and who often greatly sacrificed to do so, found himself emotionally absent from their lives.

Alcohol stole normalcy from my family's life. It is not normal to fear that your dad will stagger down the hall to meet your date. It is not normal to rescue your mom from threats of violence. It's not normal to sit on your dad's chest all night, singing to him, to keep him from hanging himself in the garage.

I had very mixed feelings for my father. At times he was a wonderful father. He provided well for our family. He drove long distances to take me to dance recitals and gymnastics meets. He bragged about my accomplishments and told me he loved me. But other times he wounded me deeply.

In junior college I recommitted my life to Jesus. God, in his love, started to teach me about himself. I learned that I was a daughter of the King and that God wanted me to cry out to him, "*Abba*, Father" (Galatians 4:6). *Abba* is an intimate word for father that means "dearest father."

By an act of my will, day after day, I have chosen to believe God's description of himself. In believing that I am secure in my Abba-Father's love, I have found the power to forgive, love and extend unconditional grace to my earthly father. Because my Father in heaven has drawn me closer to himself, I have drawn closer to my own dad. The love of my Father in heaven has given me the ability to see and respond to the best in my dad who raised me.

GOD IS RELIABLE

One of my favorite chapters in the Bible is Genesis 15, in which God makes a covenant with Abram (later Abraham). God asked Abram to bring a heifer, a goat, a ram, a dove and a pigeon. Abram cut them in two and placed them end to end. When a covenant was made in biblical times, it was a very solemn commitment. There were no loopholes. If you made a covenant, you would lock arms with the other person and walk down through the sliced-open animals. The blood of the animals would splash up and stain your skin and clothes. You were saying, "If I fail to keep this covenant with you, you may do to me what has been done to these animals."

God knew that Abram was human and would fail, so he put Abram to sleep and walked through the animals himself in the form of a smoking firepot and a blazing torch (Genesis 15:17). God made a covenant with himself. If God fails to keep his promises, he will cease to exist. We know that he is eternal and immortal and cannot cease to exist; therefore it is impossible for him to break his promise. "If we are faithless, He remains faithful; for He cannot deny Himself" (2 Timothy 2:13 NASB).

STEPPING OUT ON A PROMISE

One woman, compelled by her heart, believed that the world could be a better place and that God wanted her to step out and do something to reach that ideal. She regularly risked her life to lead slaves along the Underground Railroad to find freedom in the North.

On one trip she stopped at a sympathizer's home to feed and house her weary band. When she knocked, a stranger answered. Fearing capture, the woman prayed to God for a safe place to shelter her refugees. Dawn was breaking and they had to hurry. She remembered a swamp nearby. Carrying twin babies in a basket, she led the tired crew to the rushes and told them to lie down in the wet, cold marsh. She feared that the stranger had already alerted the authorities, so she didn't dare leave to try to find food. All day they lay there while she prayed for God's deliverance.

At dusk a Quaker farmer walked through the tall weeds nearby. He seemed to be muttering to himself. Then they made out his words: "My wagon stands in the barnyard of the next farm across the way. The horse is in the stable; the harness hangs on a nail." Then the man was gone. When the weary party arrived at the barnyard, not only was the wagon there, it was stocked with provisions!

Harriet Tubman was just one woman, but in the decade before the Civil War she made nineteen trips back and forth across the

Mason-Dixon line to lead an estimated three hundred slaves to freedom. Believing her actions were inspired by God, she led so many to the "Promised Land" of freedom that she was nicknamed "Black Moses."

Does life have you lying facedown in a swamp, praying for deliverance? The idealist arrives in the same swamp as everyone else, but she believes God can deliver!

My friend Jill Savage often says, "Don't look at the mountain, but look at the mountain mover." Jill's belief is one of the reasons her dream to encourage mothers turned into Hearts at Home Ministries, which hosts conferences where each year thousands of mothers come for encouragement and equipping.

"Don't look at the mountain, but look at the mountain mover."

Hearts at Home began as a dream in Jill's heart when she was a new stay-at-home mom who wanted to be the best mom possible. When she was in the teaching profession, there were all kinds of conferences available to help her improve in her career; but when she decided to stay home to be a full-time mom, she wondered, "Where does a mother go for training?" Jill longed to see motherhood professionalized and mothers given the respect and equipping they deserve.

Jill called together a few like-minded women. As they planned their first conference, one woman kept asking, "What will we do if a thousand moms show up?" The other planners would smile and think, *A thousand! No way, we're just a bunch of mommies.* On the day of the conference, they saw over a thousand mommies gather to learn how to be better moms.

Look to the mountain mover! The provisions for the God-sized dream he gave you are on the way!

LIVING IT OUT

What did you learn about God in this chapter that released one of your fears?

Over and over in the Bible, God tells his people to remember. Remembering helps us stay focused on God's ability rather than our inability. In Israel, when God performed a memorable work, they would build an altar, stone upon stone. It served as a marker to remind all who passed by of what God had done. When I need God to move, to work, to be big on my behalf, to simply be himself, I meditate on Scripture about who he is. For example, if I am fearful that a plan is coming unraveled, I look at verses about God's power, sovereignty and might. If I am hurt and losing perspective or hope, I mull over verses on God's goodness. Then I try to make a marker, a tangible reminder of a past victory of God. It gives me hope that God will win the future victory also.

Make your own "altar" to remind you of who God really is and who you really are. Put the "altar" where you will see it daily, as a tangible reminder that *God is for you!*

Here are some altar ideas:

- a poem, song or story
- a quilt, cross-stitch or calligraphy
- a painting, watercolor or sculpture
- a photo, poster or Bible cover
- a plant, flower or tree
- a plaque, plate or pottery
- a key chain, locket or ring
- a bookmark, bookend or video
- a memorial donation or scholarship fund

• a screen saver or screen frame for your computer

After you make your marker, dream a little. What God-sized dream does God have waiting for you? It begins with smaller steps of obedience. Today, something you already know, something you already do well or enjoy can be used by God to make a big difference. Turn the page and see how!

PROJECT ESTHER

" . . . for such a time as this." Esther 4:14

WHAT IS PROJECT ESTHER?

This outreach is titled "Project Esther" because God chooses the unlikely to do the impossible. Who was an unlikely candidate to singlehandedly rescue and save an entire nation? Esther—a beauty queen! How did she do it? She threw a party with a purpose (a series of dinners) that saved an entire nation from genocide. All Esther had to offer God was what was unique to her: beauty and a gift for hospitality. God can and will use any talent or gift we give him as a platform or vehicle to reach people for Christ if we just give it to him and are open to see how he might use the gift.

God chooses the unlikely to do the impossible.

DISCOVER YOUR UNIQUENESS

As I travel and speak to women's groups, I challenge women to find their unique God-given passion, then use that uniqueness as a platform to share the gospel. I encourage people to take a look back in order to go forward. Look back for spiritual markers, events, experiences, and verses that mark times that God used you or that are unique to you. For example, do you have

- a unique upbringing? Were you raised in a foreign country, in a minority culture, on a farm, in the inner city, by a single mom, in foster care, with a deaf sibling? We often take our upbringing for granted, but it may be the very gift God wants to use.

Project Esther

- some unique training? I started speaking publicly at age nine! Do you speak another language? Dance well? Know computers? music? math? science? What have you learned you could teach someone else?

- a unique pain that God can turn into a platform for ministry? Have you been abused, abandoned, had cancer, experienced loss, overcome an obstacle?

- a unique strength? It might be something you enjoy, such as decorating, baking, handcraft, fashion, handling money, a strong marriage, parenting skills, that you can now share. If you do something better or differently than the majority, you have a skill to share. For example, Bill and I have seen our marriage relationship bring more people to Jesus than almost anything else we do.

Everybody has a unique gift to offer that God can use!

USE YOUR UNIQUENESS FOR ETERNAL IMPACT

After a speaking engagement I drove international speaker and author Jill Briscoe to the airport. We began to talk about how women are so creative and gifted, and if they would simply use what they already know or are good at, people would be reached for Christ. She told me how in England a woman made it her goal to equip every woman in her ministry with the vision of hosting a party in her home for her prebelieving friends using a talent she *already* possessed. *Today's Woman*

Project Esther

had released a book on hosting Christmas parties with an evangelistic purpose. I thought, *Why not make that a year-round option?* At any time, anywhere in the world, a woman can throw a party with a purpose and make an eternal difference. I named this vision *Project Esther.* At Project Esther parties, we introduce our friends to our best friend, Jesus, using the gift(s) God has already given us.

DREAM OF HOW GOD CAN USE YOU

What are some examples of Project Esther outreaches? One of my friends, Lisa, makes amazing gingerbread houses. She also has an amazing personal testimony of overcoming. She created a set of several gingerbread houses, one for each transition she went through. The first was a fancy commercial candy house to symbolize her search for a perfect life—and a prince to rescue her. The next house was just ugly cardboard with lies written all over it: "You're stupid, ugly, unworthy;" it stood for the lies about herself that she believed before she found Christ. Then there was a beautiful white cathedral that symbolized the point that Christ entered her heart. Then came a manger scene for Christ leading her life. She gave her story, gave an invitation to receive Christ, gave out comment cards for responses, then gathered the cards and had a drawing and gave away the pretty gingerbread houses!

Entire ministries develop from simple parties with a purpose. Vonda made apple pies; Amy taught volleyball skills; Dianne focused on decorating; Kathy focused on shopping on sale; Linda decorated tables; Sharon decorated cakes, and so on. The Litteaurs developed a personality test that now is used by millions. My friend Ellie Kay was known as "The Coupon Queen"; now she is a financial expert worldwide. Anita Ren-

froe parlayed her sense of humor into a gift of parody that has
escorted her into many speaking opportunities in the general
market setting. Stormie Omartian simply prayed; now millions have been equipped to pray using her resources.

Here's an example of a party outline that our family has
used over and over. Nearly every year, at least one of my sons
holds a pizza and sports party for each of his sports teams. The
schedule runs something like this:

- icebreaker game/contest (about 5 minutes)

- video clip of pro athlete (1-2 minutes)

- testimony of a teammate (3-4 minutes)

- my son's story of faith (3-4 minutes)

- gospel presentation like "The Four Spiritual Laws" from
  Campus Crusade (about 6 minutes)

- comment cards/drawing for door prizes (3-4 minutes)

- free pizza and more games (such as basketball, which can
  run until everyone has been picked up by a parent)

In approximately thirty minutes the entire program is completed, the gospel has been clearly presented, and everyone has
had a fun time. We are always clear that the party is for "spiritual
inspiration" or "leadership training from a spiritual point of
view" because we want to be honest in our invitations.

DETAILS MAKE THE DIFFERENCE

How can you make your event successful? Gather a team to
help you. Ask some committed Christian friends to help with
food, invitations, details that day and so forth. It often works
well to have two or three friends use their unique gifts as a
package and have all of you invite your friendship circles.

Project
Esther

Once a few of us football moms pulled our gifts together and invited all our friends and all the other moms of the football team. Almost fifty showed up to an evening at one of the football mom's homes.

The real work is done in advance on your knees. Pray, pray, pray! Then invite three times as many people as you think you can fit in the space available. Not everyone will be able to come, so see the invitation as an extension of the event. Your friend might not make the event, but she might still want to talk about spiritual things when you invite her. Send a written invitation, and follow up with personal face-to-face invitation or call. The day before, do reminder calls and e-mails.

Be positive! Expect God to work. As a student in Campus Crusade, at my first team party for the swim team, my mentor said to me, "Share Christ in the power of the Holy Spirit, and leave the results to God." If one person comes, that is one more person who has had the opportunity to come to know Jesus. Your obedience and willingness has already made the party a success in God's eyes.

DO THE FOLLOW THROUGH

After the party, be sure to follow up with your guests. I encourage women to use a few simple questions to get spiritual conversations going:

- What did you think of the party?
- Which part did you like the best?
- Have you ever made the wonderful decision of inviting Christ into your heart?
- You'd like to, wouldn't you? I feel coming to know Christ personally is the best decision I ever made.

Then tell your story of faith, offer to give your friend a *Project Esther* booklet like *The Four Spiritual Laws* or *Steps to Peace with God* or even read it aloud, or share the gospel using any other method with which you are comfortable.

If all this talking intimidates you, then simply invite your friend to church or to a Bible study you attend, or offer to meet for coffee. If it is appropriate, offer personal mentoring one-on-one to address an area of need in her life such as parenting, marriage, fear or depression. Just give her what God has given you.

Contact me at www.farrelcommunications.com or pam@ farrelcommunications.com and let me know your Project Esther party plan. I'll pray! Then contact me and tell me what God did so I can rejoice with you!

INTERDEPENDENT
Sharpening Your People Skills

I am only one; but still I am one.
I cannot do everything, but still I can do something;
I will not refuse to do the something I can do.

HELEN KELLER

*A*s a young bride, Linda Shepherd enrolled in seminary with a dream to work in youth ministry. Due to overenrollment, the seminary unenrolled all married women not married to seminary husbands. Linda stopped seminary before she even started!

Then Linda's husband moved her hundreds of miles from home. Then her eighteen-month-old daughter Laura was thrown from a car during a violent crash, spent the next ten months of her life in a coma and awoke to severe disabilities—blind, paralyzed from the neck down and on life support.

Linda's life was turned upside down. But instead of feeling sorry for herself or her family, she began to write to encourage the hearts of the discouraged. Eventually she founded Right to the Heart Ministries, which includes her writing (nearly twenty books), speaking, a website for women leaders, a radio program, a Christian writers' and speakers' conference and other resources for women in ministry. Satan meant to defeat Linda, but her emotional pain and hardship only fueled her heart to help others.

One New Year's Eve, Linda began to think about all the people who were sad and downhearted during the holidays. She learned that New Year's Eve was the time of the highest suicide rate. She knew that desperate people would often sit at their computers and type cries for help into search engines. Linda thought, *I wish someone would put up a gospel presentation for those heartbroken people to find.* Then she realized, *My website already has just the kind of presentation that's needed.* Godtest, the website she launched that New Year's Eve, has had 1,000,000 visits from people seeking to know God. Two hundred thousand of them have come to faith in Christ. Another 200,000 were already Christians seeking help for depression.

Linda comments, "As I myself was suicidal over my daughter's inability to awaken from coma during our ordeal, God has drawn me to the broken-hearted. God has gifted me to teach those people how to give their broken hearts to the Lord."

FINDING HEALTHY FRIENDSHIPS

Women of influence should build their friendships on biblical principles, because biblical principles display the character of God. We need strong relationships with other people, but we also need to know the difference between healthy interdependence and destructive dependence.

Interdependence says, "I'll be there for you." Dependence says, "You can't do it without me."

Interdependence says, "I want you to change and grow." Dependence says, "I want you to stay the same as me."

Interdependence says, "If opening up our friendship is healthy, let's do it." Dependence says, "No one else can be your friend."

Interdependence says, "I'll wait until it's convenient." Dependence says, "I'll impose on you, but you'll understand; after all, you love me, don't you?"

Interdependence says, "What can I do to help you?" Dependence says, "What can you do to help me?"

Interdependence says, "I'm grateful for what you've given." Dependence says, "You owe me more."

GREET ONE ANOTHER

Many women find it difficult to meet new people. My family moved around a lot during my childhood, and wherever we went, my dear mom made me the unofficial greeter. I hated it at the time, but now I am grateful because it forced me to learn to meet new people.

When you think of the other person, you don't have time to think of yourself.

The most important aspect of greeting someone is to think of the other person first. When you think of the other person, you don't have time to think of yourself. A good example helps too. If you struggle with meeting new people or if you feel awkward in social settings, ask someone who is good at it to tell you how she does it. Better yet, ask if you can tag along in a social setting and observe her. Imitate what she says and does, through your own personality of course, and soon you will be more comfortable meeting and greeting new people.

BUILD ONE ANOTHER UP

"Encourage one another and build each other up" (1 Thessalonians 5:11).

I got a good picture of what it means to build up one another when we built our home. And I do mean that *we* built our home. When I was eight months pregnant, I was out there with my husband and our friends, hammering boards together, trying to race the stork and get a home built before our third child was born.

On the bearing walls and around doors and windows, we nailed 2 x 4s together so they could bear more weight. The building term for nailing the boards onto bearing walls is *sistering*. When we women hammer our lives together, we can help one another bear more weight and handle whatever life throws our way.

Accountability isn't a biblical word, but we find the principle of accountability in the Bible. The biblical word *exhortation* means "a calling alongside to bring out the best in another." *Admonishment* means "to put in mind"; it carries the idea of putting the right thoughts in the mind of another. Isn't that what we need? Friends who walk alongside, putting the right thoughts in mind to bring out our very best!

When I meet with my prayer partners, we use these questions to hold one another accountable and bring out the best in each other:

- Have you spent time with God daily?

- Have you thanked God today? this week?

- Have you talked to someone about God this week?

- Have you managed your time to reflect your priorities?

- Have you kept a good attitude toward your spouse and children?

- Have you said (or done) damaging things to any person this week?

- Have you forgiven all hurtful things done toward you?

- Have you succumbed to an addictive habit?

- Have you kept your mind pure of thoughts that would distract you from God's best plan for your life?

- Have you managed your money with integrity?

- Have you secretly wished for another's misfortune or coveted someone else's things or life?

- Have you manipulated someone else just for your own gain?

- Have you taken care of yourself and your health so that you can live longer and stronger for God?

- Did you tell me the truth today when I asked you these questions?

DANGEROUS GOSSIP

One summer I spent every devotional time studying the words *mouth, words, tongue* and *gossip* in the Bible. I wanted to find a simple definition of *gossip* so I could avoid it. Was I enlightened! My working definition of *gossip* came in the form of three questions to ask myself before I speak:

- Would I say this if the person were sitting here next to me?

- Do I have permission to share this?

- Can the person I tell do anything about the situation?

If I can't answer yes to all three questions, I keep my mouth shut!

Negative or positive, some stories are not ours to tell. Even good news shared can backfire. Once a friend joyously called me with the good news of a pregnancy. I jumped on the phone and called several friends who I knew would be so excited for her. Little did I know she was trying to call them to tell them herself. When she finally got through to them, they all responded with, "I know! Pam told me!" I had inadvertently robbed my friend of joy.

When someone comes to me with some tasty gossip, I try to stop it as soon as possible. My favorite tactics include changing the subject, politely explaining that I don't think I need to know the information, or recommending that the bearer of the news allow the person to tell me directly. If I am alone with the gossiper, I may explain that I think the topic would be gossip and is better left unsaid. I would not respond that way in a public setting because I don't want to embarrass the other person or add to the gossip cycle.

ADMONISHMENT OR CRITICISM

Women of influence must learn the difference between admonishment and criticism. Criticism is the kissing cousin to gossip. Admonishment is advice, instruction or warning. The goal of admonishment is to build up, strengthen or equip the person who is admonished.

We must earn the right to admonish another person. Too many people think that admonishment is a spiritual gift—wrong! Admonishment should be accompanied by a spiritual commitment of some kind. If you are going to point out a weakness in someone's life, you'd better be ready to offer to do something to help in that area, or you shouldn't say it!

We are told to restore others gently (Galatians 6:1) and to season our words with grace (Colossians 4:6). Some women are so good at godly admonishment that you go away feeling cared for and loved rather than ripped to shreds. The hearer of the admonishment may feel introspective, because the Holy Spirit is at work, but she should also feel that you said the words because you truly care for her best interests. If you want to admonish for any other reason—keep quiet!

Sometimes criticism does hit the bull's-eye. At those times I must take the remarks to the feet of Jesus and ask him to sort through them. The Word tells us to throw down vain speculations, and I know Satan is the king of liars, so I want to reject criticism that comes from him. But if the criticism holds even a grain of admonition from God, I want my heart to receive it.

Criticism leaves me feeling vulnerable. I try not to leap to my own defense. Instead I simply respond, "Thank you for sharing your heart." Then I go before the Lord with my heavy heart. After I have spent time with Jesus over the content of the criticism, I'll pray over my response to it. One day while watching TV I heard Joyce Meyer say this about criticism: "If you find yourself in a place that you are feeling hurt or discouraged by someone's smallness, jealousy, hurtful words, negativity, or unkindness, then praise God because it could be worse—you could be them!"

When I am hurt, I have several choices.

I can forgive and go on without a word. This is often my method with the continually contentious critic. Responding to criticism from some people simply fuels more criticism, because what they want is either control or attention. I prefer to give others the benefit of the doubt and forgive, assuming they weren't intentionally seeking to hurt me.

I can forgive and then set up an appointment to talk. I want to respond if my critic is young in the Lord because it gives me a good teaching opportunity, even if only to model the biblical way to admonish. I want to respond if the person and I need to be reunited for fellowship or work. I want to respond if the criticism is from a leader or supervisor; in that case I may simply correct my behavior or I may set up a conference to clarify my stand and bargain for a resolution. If I am fearful of my critic, I may want to request a meeting with a mediator, a neutral third party who can help us iron out our differences.

Don't allow criticism to sidetrack you from God's plan for you.

Before any confrontation, I seek to set up as many guidelines as possible. Whose issue is this—yours, mine, both, someone else's? Who needs to be at the meeting? Where shall we meet? How long shall we meet? You don't want to cause a dispute over the meeting itself. I suggest that you pray and set up some parameters for the meeting, then offer the guidelines to your critic. If you can't agree, ask for a mediator to arrange the parameters as well.

If you are a woman of influence, expect criticism. Those who rest comfortably back in the barracks aren't on the firing line as you are. When you are a woman of influence, you make things happen. When you make things happen, you stir up the status quo, and some people will respond with criticism. Whatever you do, don't allow the criticism to sidetrack you from God's plan for you.

In doing God's will, your heart will be healed.

Early in my ministry I received a long letter full of attacks on my character, my motives, my ministry and my family. The letter arrived after a long stretch of exhausting work, when I was vulnerable to discouragement. As I read the letter, a dark cloud covered my heart. I cried out to God in my hurt. Then I got angry. Then I cried. Then I got depressed. I felt as if I were in an emotional knockdown, drag-out fight. Satan wanted me so discouraged that I couldn't minister. And believe me, my flesh felt like giving in. I knew I could choose a bitter place or a broken place. It's natural to want to turn bitter. It's better to be broken over a hurt and allow God to heal it.

It took several months, but gradually my perspective returned. In my brokenness, I continued to do what God had called me to do. As I kept my eyes on Jesus and the needs of others, I gained a new and bolder resolve. When someone hurts or attacks you, keep doing what you know to be your calling, your passion and your path. In doing God's will, your heart will be healed.

FORGIVE ONE ANOTHER

Forgiveness is necessary for any ongoing healthy relationship. Forgiveness doesn't mean that you forget that a wrong was done or belittle the issue. Forgiveness doesn't say, "Oh, that's okay." A wrong inflicted is not okay! Forgiveness is a decision of my will to stop the effect of injustice on the development of my character.

To help people understand forgiveness, my husband Bill created a set of six statements that we use in our speaking and counseling ministry.

Forgiveness says:

1. I forgive _____ (person) for _____ (offense).

2. I admit that what was done was wrong.

3. I do not expect _____ (person) to make up for what he/she has done.

4. I will not use this offense to define who _____ (person) is.

5. I will not manipulate _____ (person) with the offense.

6. I will not allow the offense to stop my growth.

Jesus does not expect us to make up for our sin. That would be impossible. Neither does he dismiss our sin as unimportant. He does not rationalize it or whitewash it. He died for it! We cannot undo what we have done wrong, but we can accept God's forgiveness and go on to live out a healthy life with godly behavior.

Jesus does not define us by our sin. When we come to him, we are made new creations. God sees us clothed in Christ's righteousness. Jesus doesn't manipulate us with our sin. He doesn't hang it over our head or stab us in the back with it. He gives us a clean slate. He frees us to grow into all he designed us to be.

GET ALONG WITH ONE ANOTHER

An old man sat on the front porch of a town's general store. A couple drove up and engaged him in conversation. "Hi, we are new to this community. What's it like here?"

"Well," said the old man, "what was it like where you came from?"

"People were so nice and friendly, kind and loving."

"Well, that's pretty much how you'll find them here."

A while later, another couple moving to town stopped by. "Hi, we are new to this community. What's it like here?"

"Well," said the old man, "what was it like where you came from?"

"People were cold and critical and gossipy and grumpy."

"Well, that's pretty much how you'll find them here."

We help create the relationships we have.

The golden rule definitely applies: "Do to others what you would have them do to you" (Matthew 7:12). The Bible tells us to bear with, live in harmony with, accept and have *A humble heart forgives readily.* compassion on one another. The key principle for choosing to get along is found in Ephesians 4:2: "Be completely humble and gentle; be patient, bearing with one another in love." In 1 Peter 5:5 we are reminded to "clothe yourselves with humility toward one another."

A humble heart doesn't have to always be right. A humble heart doesn't care who gets the glory—except God. A humble heart is not easily offended. A humble heart has learned that the secret to great leadership is servanthood. A humble heart seeks the greatest good of all. A humble heart can lovingly agree to disagree. A humble heart forgives readily. A humble heart majors on the majors and minors on the minors.

A top-ranking British official once entertained a haughty and sophisticated lady in his home. By mistake, the host's assistant asked her to sit on the left of her host rather than at the place of honor at his right. The visitor was offended and became indignant. Turning to the general, who was her host, she said, "I suppose you have real difficulty in getting your aide-de-camp to seat guests properly at the table."

"Oh, not at all," replied the general. "I have found that those that matter don't mind, and those that mind don't matter."

BE STRETCHER-BEARER FRIENDS

When someone is injured in a battle, the wounded person is loaded onto a stretcher and carried to a place of help. Stretcher-bearers are the handful of people you would call on if something awful happened in your life. You *know* you can depend on them. We all need them, and we need to *be* them for others. Luke tells the story of a man who was carried and then lowered through a roof so Jesus could help him. Seeing their faith—the faith of the friends—Jesus healed the man (Luke 5:17-26).

Who could you call if something happened to you, your husband, your child or your parents? Which friends would offer the kind of wisdom, consolation and support that you would need?

All the friends whom I would call in an emergency are friends to whom I have had to say "I'm sorry." These friends know I don't have it all together. They have seen me at my worst. They know my shortcomings and accept me anyway. They are committed to seeing that I stay on track until I arrive at the finish line.

Such relationships are rare. My stretcher-bearer friends are worth sacrificing for in order to keep in touch with them. And I have found the best way to get stretcher-bearer friends is to be one.

ACCEPT ONE ANOTHER

I was meeting with a woman I discipled. I sat and explained the next steps that I thought she should take in her growth as a leader. I rattled off plans and ideas. With every idea of mine, she would respond, "Pam, I don't think I can do this." And I would reply with a pep talk. Eventually this quiet woman looked me straight in the eye and said with as much resolve as she could, "You're not listening to me! I'm saying I can't do that right now!"

Then I finally heard her. She was not philosophically opposed to any of the plan. She'd been trying to explain an inner conflict, and I was downplaying it. I had always been her cheerleader. She had always been able to look to me for acceptance and support. Now, when she really needed me, I was dumping unrealistic expectations on her.

I was pushing my agenda for her, rather than supporting the agenda God had for her. I apologized, backed off and listened.

We must help people get to God's place for them, not *our* place for them. Sometimes it will be the same place, sometimes not. God is the best one to help your friend find his will for her own life. Her job is to listen to God. Your job is to help her stay plugged in to God.

> *We must help people get to God's place for them, not our place for them.*

INSTRUCT ONE ANOTHER

Our future leaders must be well taught. How can we expect a person to do a job if the person has never been trained? A woman of influence desires to share where she has been so others can be equipped to get to God's destination.

In *A Chance to Die,* Elisabeth Elliot tells how she was influenced by the life of Amy Carmichael:

Amy Carmichael became for me what some now call a role model. She was far more than that. She was my spiritual mother. She showed me the shape of godliness. For a time, I suppose, I thought she must have been perfect, and that was good enough for me. As I grew up I knew she could not have been perfect, and that was better, for it meant that I might possibly walk in her footprints. If we demand perfect role models we will have, except for the Son of Man himself, none at all.

BE HOSPITABLE TO ONE ANOTHER

Our homes should be an extension of our influence. Our society is so mobile that often we don't know our neighbors—or even try to. We commute to work, and the last thing we want to do when we get home is entertain.

There lies a fallacy. Hospitality is not entertaining. Hospitality is an attitude of opening up your life so that others can come in. There are three objections to overcome if you want to be a hospitable person: (1) I don't have enough time, (2) I don't have enough money, (3) I don't have enough space. Notice that all three statements begin with I. By contrast, hospitality begins with *you*.

Hospitality is an attitude of opening up your life so that others can come in.

No time. A hospitable person learns to party as she goes. If it is important to you, you will creatively carve out time. Take snacks for the car pool. Grab a pile of magazines, tie them with a bow and drop them off for a friend. On the way to work, get two mochas and chat with a coworker for a few minutes. Keep a "party box" supplied with crepe paper streamers, balloons, tape, posterboard and markers; you can use these at short notice to celebrate somebody.

No money. The best party I ever gave was a birthday celebration for Bill while we were in seminary. We were broke, and so were all our seminary friends. I sent out invitations written on brown paper lunch bags. The recipients were asked to fill the bags with their favorite snacks as their gifts to Bill. At the party I put out a bunch of art supplies, tape and scissors, and each person was asked to create a gift for Bill out of another brown lunch bag. The gifts were a riot. He got bags for under his eyes, a brown paper briefcase, brown paper sunglasses, a brown paper suit. I provided popcorn and drinks. I'm sure the entire party cost well under ten dollars—maybe under five!

No space. My mom used to tell me, "People are coming to see us, not the house." If your dorm room or apartment or house is not large enough for an event, just move the party! Go to the park, the beach, the lake, the garage, the yard, the driveway, the community center or the barn! One creative couple I knew lived in a tiny studio apartment, so they would offer to cook elaborate meals and take them to the homes of their friends. All their friends loved it, because they lived hectic dual-career lives and seldom got a home-cooked meal!

REDEFINING RELATIONSHIPS

Relationships will change along the way. There are "friends of the heart and friends for the road." Some relationships are permanent, while others are meant only for a season.

There are "friends of the heart and friends for the road."

I continually weigh before the Lord which women I need to spend time with. When I know the purpose for a relationship, I can evaluate whether it is meant to be permanent or temporary. I have discovered that my relationships need to be redefined each time there is a significant change. One of us may move, get a new job, have a baby or whatever. When you are honest in relationships, your friends will be free to respond with known expectations, rather than tied in knots wondering where they stand with you.

Sometimes people want more from you than you can give, or more than you feel God wants you to give. It is better to be honest and tactfully explain your limitations than to promise something you cannot give or have no intention of giving. I ask the person to tell me where she sees the relationship going from this point, and I share my view as well.

Sometimes people step out of my life and it has nothing to do with me. If the person has been a close friend, a colleague or a disciple, I try to find out if she is struggling with a personal or spiritual problem. For some women, I can only drop a quick note in the mail or leave a brief message on voicemail. But if I can, I try to have a face-to-face redefinition. I always try to be loving and upbeat and to really listen. I try not to burn any bridges that I might need to walk back over.

As you redefine a relationship, review how God called your friendship into existence. Focus on the special needs that the friendship addressed for the season. Elaborate the positive qualities that each of you brought to the relationship at the time.

When you have to redefine a friendship with another believer, focus on God's sovereignty and care. When you have to redefine a relationship with an unbeliever or in a secular work setting, drop all the Christian language. Refrain from telling people that God called you to leave them. They could interpret it as some weird channeling experience or take it to mean that God doesn't like them. Your relationship may have to change, but try to keep the door open for their connection to God.

SERVE ONE ANOTHER

The best leaders are first the best servants. We have to know how to follow well in order to know how to lead well. Jesus said, "Whoever wants to be first must be last of all and servant of all" (Mark 9:35 NRSV).

The servant's attitude goes against everything the world teaches us. We're supposed to look out for number one, go for the jugular. We don't get a lot of praise for serving. We may even have to fight the feeling that others are taking advantage of us.

It was Easter morning and it was raining. I got my two toddlers ready for this special day and then went to get dressed myself. I came out of my bedroom and found the two boys stomping in mud puddles on the patio. I called them in, but Zach was reluctant, so I went out in the rain after him. He reached up for me to carry him and promptly marched his muddy feet up my new white skirt.

I cried out, "Zach, please stop!"

"Why?" asked Zach.

"This skirt is special. Mommy is a person too!"

Then Brock chimed in, "You're not a person—you're a mommy!"

Author Colleen Townsend Evans says the best way to test your servant spirit is to notice how you react when you are treated like a servant. My servant's heart wasn't too healthy that day, but my sons helped me realize that a servant's heart sees a need and seeks to meet that need without personal gain.

Living It Out

Do you have a balanced assortment of relationships? Are all your friends non-Christians or all Christians? Do you need to deepen some relationships or make new ones? Choose one of these friendship-building activities:

1. Personally thank those who are your stretcher-bearers.

2. Schedule time with a person with whom you'd like a deeper friendship.

3. Make a list of places you can meet new friends. Meet someone new this week.

4. Redefine a relationship by meeting with that person.

5. Write thank-you cards to everyone who has offered help along your path.

6. Sometimes our friendship network needs balance. Ask yourself who is missing from your circle of friends. Do you have mentors? mentees (people for whom you are a mentor)? stretcher-bearer friends? those who are seeking God? cheerleaders (encouragers)?

6

INITIATIVE
Reaching Your Potential

Do not follow where the path may lead.
Go instead where there is no path and leave a trail.

MURIEL STRODE

*N*o!" the woman shouted almost instinctively as she rose to her feet. The sound echoed through the meeting hall. An assembly of delegates had just vetoed her husband's request to be employed as an itinerant pastor for the movement. She was shocked. She was so sure this was God's will for herself and her husband. At first she was filled with deep frustration at what appeared to be a serious roadblock to their dream. Then she was struck with the realization that this was God's permission for them to fly. God had other plans, bigger plans for them. Both of them sensing God's leading, the couple joined hands and left the building.

Catherine and William Booth walked away from an opportunity to minister in one location where they would earn a somewhat secure income and keep the successful ministry they already had achieved. They felt a call to minister to all of England, especially to the poorest and most downtrodden. That day the Booths left the known and stepped into the unknown to launch a ministry that would become the Salvation Army.

Catherine had been a sickly and fragile child, unable to attend traditional school for most of her life. Instead of wasting her time feeling sorry for herself, she flooded her mind with great literature. By the time she was twelve, she had read the Bible eight times, and she loved the classics, everything from Dickens to Dante.

She married the bright and articulate, though poorly educated, William Booth, and they launched into a life characterized by faith, risk and servanthood. Catherine didn't wait to be invited to speak. One day after William had preached, she asked if she might say a few words. William consented, and the result was a stirring sermon that moved the hearts of the congregation for a second time that morning. It also broke down a barrier. At the time it was unusual for women to speak publicly in England, but news of Catherine's inspirational gift spread. She was as talented in the pulpit as was her itinerant preacher husband. Both drew huge crowds throughout England.

Catherine was a dedicated mother who raised eight children. She didn't wait for her children to grow up before she ministered. She took them to do ministry with her. All eight went on to leadership positions within the Salvation Army.

Catherine Booth felt that life was too short to wait around. She looked for ways to make a difference; and if she didn't find any, she created them. She felt that much of what society wanted women to do was a waste of their time and talents. Years later she wrote in a letter to one of her children, "We are made for larger ends than earth can compass. Oh let us be true to our exalted destiny." Frustrated by the material frivolity she saw around her, she said, "It will be a happy day for England, when Christian ladies transfer their attention from poodles and terriers to destitute and starving children." Under Catherine's leadership, many women did just that!

Later in life, Catherine Booth threw herself into a political battle over the selling of young girls for prostitution. In England there was no penalty for pimping girls. If the girl was younger than thirteen, she was too young to testify. If she was over thirteen, she was at the age of consent, and all girls were treated as if they had consented!

Catherine appealed to the Queen. After several years of trying to raise the awareness of the public, she saw a new law passed that raised the age of consent to eighteen. The law made it a criminal offense to seduce or procure women for immoral purposes, gave authorities searching rights, and made men and women equal under the law because it was equally criminal to solicit men or women. When Catherine died, fifty thousand mourners filed past to pay their respects to a woman who had helped a generation believe God for a better life.

A woman of initiative knows where she is going and is excited about taking others with her. Passion without particulars is just emotion. Passion will lay the foundation, but initiative lays the bricks, builds the walls and finishes off the house where hope can live.

STEP UP

In Scripture, God gives us many promises that if we trust him, he will guide us and strengthen us. If we do the known, he will lead us through the unknown.

"Trust in the LORD with all your heart and lean not on your own understanding; in all your ways acknowledge him, and he will make your paths straight" (Proverbs 3:5-6).

"Delight yourself in the LORD and he will give you the desires of your heart. Commit your way to the LORD; trust in him and he will do this: He will make your righteousness shine like the dawn, the justice of your cause like the noonday sun" (Psalm 37:4-6).

"Commit your work to the LORD, and your plans will be established" (Proverbs 16:3 NRSV).

To be a woman of influence, you must have goals. Goals do not have to be intimidating. Are you terrified each time you climb a flight of stairs? Of course not! Goals are like a stairway. One after another, the steps will get you from where you are now to where you want to be.

Let's say that right now you are the mother of two preschoolers, ages four and three. In two years both children will be in school, at least from 8 a.m. to 12 p.m. You have completed two years of college, and you dream of finishing your degree and running your own business. You pray with your family and decide that a home-based business would provide needed income and eventually give you the flexibility to return to school and finish your education.

Goals are like a stairway.

You now have a long-term goal; but in order to get there, you need to reach a series of short-term goals. To identify them, brainstorm a list of what you need to do to get your business off the ground. Don't worry about chronological order yet. For example,

• pray with family

• talk to professionals in the field I'd like to work in

• go to a business fair

• make connections in SCORE (retired business professionals)

• contact Chamber of Commerce for information on laws (many have new business packets)

• (check out home business books from the library

• check out home business information and newsletters on the Internet

- obtain financial information
- make a business plan
- secure financing and supplies
- set up workspace
- plan advertising or public relations

Now make a stairway of short-term goals. Arrange the steps in the order you think they need to happen, with the beginning steps at the bottom. For example, you may want to research the job field and talk to professionals early, because the market may be sluggish or a new development may be under way. After you have put each step into the stairway, place a target date next to the step. Now you have an orderly plan to climb upward to your goal. Your staircase might look like this:

September: Launch business.

August: Create a business plan; secure capital/resources.

July: Narrow choices and investigate details.

June: Contact Chamber of Commerce and SCORE; investigate financial leads.

May: Attend business fair; talk to others in business area of interest.

April: Pray with family; determine budget and financial need; network with other women in business; read books, newsletters, magazines and journals.

YOUR PLAN

Emilie Barnes writes, "Goals are just dreams with deadlines." Do you have dreams waiting to be fulfilled? Are you a student? newly married? planning a wedding? setting goals for your children or your marriage? Is a job change or career reentry ahead? Are you looking toward an empty nest or retirement?

Identify one specific dream. Brainstorm a list of things that need to happen in order to achieve your dream. Take your list and plug the ideas into a stairstep diagram such as the one below:

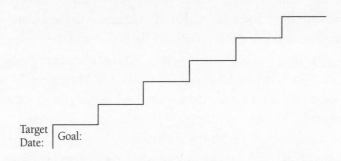

Target
Date: | Goal:

You now have a workable plan for achieving your dream. Of course you may need to make adjustments along the way. Some steps may turn out to be unnecessary. You may need to do other steps that you did not anticipate. The steps may happen in a different order than you expect. But you have a place to begin and you have an end goal in mind.

"Goals are just dreams with deadlines."

Look Within

In order to maintain a balanced life, it is helpful to set goals in four major areas: Spiritual life, Team, Energy, and Productivity. Develop your individual S.T.E.P. plan as follows:

S: Your spiritual life. In this area you will want to write goals for your relationship with God. Consider your prayer life, Bible study, quiet time, Scripture memorization, church attendance, fasting, corporate worship, small group connections and so on. The key to a rich spiritual life is to consistently "be filled with the Spirit" (Ephesians

5:18). When a woman is filled with the Holy Spirit, she is yielding to God's rule in her life.

My dear friend Marjorie has endured abandonment by her husband, the death of her only son, the loss of a career position shortly before retirement and a home that burned nearly to the ground. She amazes me with her ability to bounce back after such severe trauma. Right after the fire, I took Marjorie shopping for a few necessities. She told me, "Pam, the Bible says in the end it'll all burn anyway; mine just went up a little sooner than yours." As we hugged and laughed in the crisp Christmas air, I realized I was standing in the presence of a woman whose spiritual life was vibrant.

T: *Your team.* This area includes goals that affect the people closest to you: your spouse, children, parents, friends, the person you are dating and so on. You and another person may agree on the goal ("My husband and I will go out on a date each Thursday") or you may set the goal personally ("I will send a special card in each of my children's lunches once a week").

Limit your team goals to things over which you have a degree of control. For example, you may want a happier marriage and think the quickest route is to fix your husband. The problem is, you have no control over your husband. You have the ability to change only yourself and must trust God to work with your mate.

You may have a goal of becoming closer friends with someone. It's a good goal as long as you realize you cannot control the friend's involvement in your relationship. You can carve out time to spend with a friend and decide to encourage her, but you can't dictate her response.

It is especially important to guard your sexual purity, whether you are single or married. One indiscretion can wipe out years of influence. It is God's will that we should avoid sexual immorality (1 Thessalonians 4:3). Premarital sex, homosexuality and adultery are not options for the woman of influence. If you are single, define your own boundaries before you enter a dating relationship, and discuss them early in the relationship. Confiding your boundaries to a friend or mentor will help you remain true to your convictions. If you are married, encourage your mentor and close friends to ask you about your thought life, your romantic relationship and your feelings toward your husband. The uniqueness and privacy of the marriage should be protected, but make yourself accountable in this area.

This is also the place to identify goals concerning your mothering, your role as a daughter, an in-law or any other relationship you would like to see grow. You can even include ideas for activities, romantic dates, birthday celebrations or anything else that will help promote close relationships.

E: Your energy. This area includes issues that involve your personal well-being, such as physical health, emotional development, hobbies or social needs. This area may also address goals that range from wardrobe needs to counseling or support group assignments—whatever will help you be well enough or have enough energy to accomplish the goals you have set in the other areas of your life.

We have to take care of ourselves if we are to maintain our influence in the lives of others. Daisy Hepburn advises women, "Do first that which only *you* can do." I know that I'm the only one who can exercise for me or read for me. I am also the only mother my boys will ever have. Only I can be my husband's wife and lover. Everything else has to follow.

Sometimes the best thing you can do to take care of yourself is to "do nothing." Some days when the sun is hot and bright and the ocean beckons me, I throw the beach bag in the car with a few snacks and drinks, pick up the kids from school and head straight to the beach for a few hours while everyone else is doing homework. Definite goals for personal energy let you be spontaneous and guilt-free about taking time for yourself, because you know when and where to jump back on track.

P: *Your productivity*. In this area your goals can include plans for career, education and ministry. Ministry plans will include personal areas of influence, such as discipleship or church leadership, as well as any public ministry plans, such as being in charge of a ministry or running special events. If you are in management or own your own business, you include your business plan in this goal. You will be more productive day by day when you have a clear plan of action.

In college I was on the springboard diving team and a student leader in Campus Crusade for Christ. During my first diving season, the two never conflicted. In fact my diving furthered my ministry. By the end of the season I had shared Christ with the entire women's team and most of the men's team. Sharing Jesus helped me overcome my fear of people; getting back up and trying again after hitting the water—*hard*—helped me overcome the fear of failure.

During my second diving season, about half the meets were moved from Fridays to Tuesdays. Tuesdays were Campus Crusade leadership training, ministry planning and Bible study nights. The first Tuesday I missed Bible study. The second Tuesday I arrived late. As I saw the next Tuesday coming up, I knew I had to choose. I talked with the woman who was discipling me; I talked with the woman who had discipled her; I talked with a Christian coach; I talked with my friends and my parents. There was no consensus. After church on Sunday, I grabbed my Bible and went off to talk with God. The sermon had been from the book of 1 John so I decided to start there. I got stopped in my tracks by 1 John 2:15-17: "Do not love the world or anything in the world. If anyone loves the world, the love of the Father is not in him. For everything in the world—the cravings of sinful man, the lust of his eyes and the boasting of what he has and does—comes not from the Father but from the world. The world and its desires pass away, but the man who does the will of God lives forever."

God made me take a long hard look at why I was diving. It wasn't to stay in shape; I had three physical education classes and I was a gymnastics instructor. It wasn't to share my faith; I'd already shared with everyone I could. I was diving for me. I had come to enjoy the glory of winning and the delight of center stage. I also liked the tan! I knew I was not good enough to get a diving scholarship to further my education. Diving was interfering with new challenges of ministry God was presenting to me. For me, diving had now become the wrong choice.

I made personal appointments with all my coaches and explained my decision. Some took it well; some didn't. I talked to the members of my team and explained my decision and offered my continued support and friendship. In a very short time, I was put in leadership positions in ministry where I learned the foundational skills that are vital to me today.

Corrie ten Boom is one of my ministry role models. She was part of a dedicated Christian family who hid Jews during the Holocaust, and she spent years in a concentration camp for her love of the Jewish people. Her writing has had a profound effect on me. One day this simple paragraph grabbed my attention: "When a house is on fire and you know that there are people in it, it is a sin to straighten pictures in that house. When the world about you is in great danger, works that are in themselves not sinful can become quite wrong."

As you set goals for your own work and ministry, make this your prayer: *Lord, help me clarify my purpose by seeing the state of the world through your eyes.*

LOOK AHEAD

Goals are our attempt to take the priorities God lays out in his Word and the twenty-four hours he gives us each day and make the best use of them. Goals are not rules! Goals are just guidelines to your dreams. The overarching aim in writing goals is to plan enough to accomplish the best of what God has planned for you, yet be flexible enough to change so that you accomplish the best of what God has for you. Even though I have goals, each day is held up to God with open hands and the prayer "Not my will but thy will."

Try to picture yourself in ten years. How old will you be? How old will your husband or children or parents be? Their life stages will affect you. If you are single, what dreams would you like to see fulfilled, even if you do not marry? What character traits would you like to develop? What wisdom, knowledge or training would you like to receive? What kind of person would you like to become? Weigh out your heart's desire before the Lord, then write some goals for the long term. Note in the margin with a $ any goals that cost money; at the bottom of your goal sheet, total the cost and note any financial goals that you need to add in order to finance your other goals.

Here is an example of a long-term spiritual life goal:

By the time I am forty-five I want to have read through the Bible five more times.

After you have written your long-term goals, take each one and write out specific steps you'll need to take in the next two to five years to accomplish that goal. Choose a consistent target date for all your goals (by the time I am twenty, thirty, forty, fifty and so on). Now complete your list of short-term goals and the financial impact of each. For example,

By the time I am forty-five I want to have read through the Bible using two study resources: the *Inductive Study Bible* and the *Quiet Time Bible Guide*.

For some people January represents a fresh start. Summer is my own emotional fresh start. For my family the school year has such a huge impact that prior to the opening of school we all reevaluate. In late August I write my goals for the upcoming year.

Whatever time of year you choose for your reevaluation time, ask yourself: Am I chipping away at the goals that are most important to me? Is there anything I can delegate to someone else, to get it done better or more quickly? Can I eliminate one responsibility before I take on another? Complete your list of goals, remembering to note the financial implications. Be very specific! For example,

> This year I will do a study of leaders and leadership principles as I read through the Bible at least once in my devotional times daily. I will memorize verses to help strengthen me as a leader at the pace of one per week.

I keep a copy of my goals posted in my office. I also keep a copy of the boys' "Learner and Leader" goals for the year, as well as a sheet with Bill's top priorities that affect me. I use Outlook on my laptop and sync with my PDA phone to stay on track. You can also use paper organizational systems. Just try to keep your priorities in front of you so you can move forward with your goals.

It helps to set up natural review times every few months to see how you are progressing. I usually use my wedding anniversary, my birthday and one day of summer vacation as natural reevaluation times. I try to carve out longer quiet times with God, heart-to-heart talks with Bill and one-on-one time with the boys. I pencil in an average weekly schedule at this time as a visual aid to show whether I am overbooking my life. Bill and I compare schedules and make adjustments.

When you write down goals, be sure that you also schedule time to accomplish the goals. Writing out a general weekly schedule makes your goals a natural part of your life. For example, when our children were young, bedtime was marked out in a one-hour block to include showers, Bible reading and devotions, family read-aloud of a literary classic, and time to chat with each child about his day. In order to attain the goals of family devotions and reading, we had to make them a regular part of our schedule.

Once a week Bill and I set aside a morning to coordinate calendars and check up on the important goals. I come into this meeting with a list of questions and my ASAP list. We tie this to a weekly workout/ exercise date followed by breakfast. This is in addition to our weekly romantic date time. We protect our "date night" time because talking about the business/problem-solving side of life can squelch the romantic mood! So we have two dates a week: one for fun and one for work.

Once a week we have a family meeting. Everyone brings their schedule and their list of priorities for the week. We have a master family calendar with each person's schedule color-coded. (You can buy calendars with larger spaces for writing, designed to handle multiple people's schedules.) The kids' major responsibilities are also on my Outlook because a science fair project or a term paper may demand my time if one of the kids needs help.

Each evening I preview the next day and make my to-do list. Then Bill and I have a five-minute meeting to update, make changes and exchange new information. Each morning after my devotions, I run through my to-do list and reprioritize, delegate or drop things off my list.

If you use a weekly schedule, you can write at the top your focus for each day. Note your husband's and children's priorities as well. At the bottom, write your daily imperative. If your day spins out of control, what one thing do you need to accomplish that day, even if you can't do anything else? For example, on Thursday my imperative is finding some romantic time with Bill. On Monday it is cleaning the house—even if only the living room, kitchen and bath—because Sunday usually means company at our house. When we built our home, Bill was basically working two full-time jobs. The daily imperative was a lifesaver because it made sure that what was most crucial for our marriage and for our children still happened, no matter what.

Included at the end of this chapter is a budget worksheet, because finances that spin out of control will seriously impede your ability to reach your goals.

If you will tenaciously apply these steps in your journey, you will initiate and achieve your goals. You will become a woman of initiative who really can get things done. God wants you to feel a sense of accomplishment. He knows you are a champion. He tells you, "Run in such a way that you may win" (1 Corinthians 9:24 NASB). Together you and God can set a winning course.

LIVING IT OUT

Write out your long-term, short-term and yearly goals. In pencil, mark out your average weekly schedule. Having goals will help you reach for the S.T.A.R.S! Ask yourself these questions:

- Specific: Can you measure progress so you will know when you've reached it?

- Tangible: Have you written it down and scheduled it into your daily life?

- Attainable by faith: Is it a stretch, so you need God's power?

- Reachable: Do you have a measure of control, meaning you can do something about it?

- Shared: Have you run your plan by those it will affect or who will join to help you achieve it (spouse, kids, parents, mentors)?

If God planted the dream, he will eventually plant the plan to financially underwrite the dream. We must be wise stewards of the dream and the dream's financial plan. Look at how your finances add up and how well they reflect your goals. For the following worksheet, look back over the past twelve months and find the average monthly amount that you have been spending in each category.

MONTHLY BUDGET WORKSHEET

Income

Salaries:

Other:

Total income:

Expenses

Tithe:

Taxes:

Housing (all expenses, including rent or mortgage, insurance, up-keep, decorating, all utilities):

Groceries:

Auto (car payments, gas, upkeep, insurance, tax and license):

Insurance (life, health and any other insurance):

Debt (all debt, excluding mortgage and monthly minimum payments):

Entertainment/Recreation (eating out, tickets, video rental, any other activity, plus a monthly vacation savings amount):

Work Expenses (childcare costs; any professional expenses):

Clothing (monthly dollar figure for each family member):

Savings/Retirement:

Medical Expenses (any copayments, medical or dental bills not covered by insurance; monthly cost of prescriptions and over-the-counter medications):

Miscellaneous (personal care needs—haircuts, cosmetics, dry cleaning; personal allowance for each family member; unreimbursed ministry expenses; gifts; educational costs; hobbies; postage; photos; magazines and so on):

Total expenses:

Subtract expenses from income:

If income exceeds expenses, plan how to invest or give away the surplus. If expenses exceed income, plan quick action to cut expenses, raise income or both. A wise woman taught me, "If your outgo exceeds your income, then your upkeep will become your downfall." Ellie Kay's *A Woman's Guide to Family Finances* will help you with many more financial decisions.

7

INTEGRITY
Consistent Living in an Inconsistent World

It is never too late to be what you might have been.

GEORGE ELIOT

$\mathcal{T}$he words just rolled out of Natalie's mouth. Her boss wanted her to use a business practice that Natalie thought was unethical. Natalie prayed, *God, help me—I need an answer now! I want all my life to glorify you.* Then the words sprang from her heart and into the conversation: "I just can't do that!"

The air was tense. Natalie knew she had to stand her ground, but she was concerned about being sensitive to those around her. *What if they don't understand? Am I being too tough? Am I saying this in a way that will glorify you, Lord?*

Natalie had rededicated her life to Christ a few years before. She had steadily grown in her relationship with Christ. Because she was a manager, she felt a responsibility to the women who worked under her, some of whom were nonbelievers or young believers.

"I stood my ground and refused to compromise," Natalie shared with excitement, "and my sales went up!" A few months later, she felt that perhaps God wanted her to cut back her work hours for the sake of her family and ministry priorities. She decided not to work on weekends except during a few big marketing weeks. Her sales went up again! Then she was asked to be a support person in a counseling ministry. The commitment would tie her up every other Wednesday evening for several months. Wednesday nights were some of her big sales times. She felt God impressing her to take on the ministry. Her sales went up once again! Within weeks she was the top salesperson in the distributorship. Reflecting on the success, Natalie states emphatically, "I knew God would be there for me, if I was there for him."

Integrity is a commitment to live consistently with what you know to be true about life. I have taught my children, "Integrity is who you are when no one is looking except God." A woman of influence weaves integrity into her life ahead of time so that, when pressed for a decision, she will decide the right thing to do on the spot.

Integrity is who you are when no one is looking except God.

Integrity opens doors for influence because people learn to trust you.

SOMETIMES INTEGRITY COSTS

"Sandra, you can no longer help those people from your church with their financial needs. You are forbidden to give any financial advice outside the walls of this institution. It's a conflict of interest. Take your choice—it's this job or your volunteer work."

Sandra had gone through a huge financial downturn due to a divorce. She was sensitive to women who needed financial counseling.

Most were widows on fixed incomes who couldn't afford to pay for financial advice or who were overwhelmed with the new responsibility of managing their money. Sandra's pastor asked her to help some of them. She volunteered to help others.

Several times Sandra tried to explain to her boss that she had crossed no legal boundaries and that she felt ethically obligated to help those less fortunate. After battling with the decision for many months, she quit the company. Her heart wasn't with money; it was with people. She held several part-time positions while she prayed that God would provide her with a full-time position where she could use her talents *and* help people.

Then Sandra was approached by a company that specialized in the needs of the elderly. They needed someone with her skills and a heart for the older generation. They approached her because she had a reputation for helping older women *and* she had a reputation as a woman of integrity.

HOLY FOR HIM

The word *holy* may bring up the image of nuns' habits and a life cloistered away from the real world. But holiness isn't only for those inside the walls of a protected community. Holiness is for every child of God.

Holiness is for every child of God.

Let's say you come to my house for dinner and I offer you something to drink. I set before you two crystal goblets, both beautifully etched, both containing the same water. However, one goblet has impurities floating in it—a dead fly, some dirt, bits of leftover food. The water in the other goblet is sparkling clean. Which glass will you choose? The sparkling clean one, I hope!

It is the same with God. When he looks around for whom to use for the honorable task of representing him, he wants a pure container. If we refuse to deal with our sins, if we have specifically disobeyed God's will, we are like the impure glass. So often we pray, *God, use me,* but we don't want to go through the cleansing process to become usable.

How Do I Handle Temptation?

During high school I had the opportunity to visit the city morgue. We trailed along behind our forensic guide. As we entered the morgue, I was stunned by the sight. Bodies lay on gurneys about the room, tags on their toes, covered by white sheets. Everything was quiet until one young woman blurted out, "I think I need to leave!" and dashed out of the room. Not one of the corpses heard her.

I think of those corpses when I read in Romans 6:11 that we are dead to sin. Dead people do not respond. It doesn't matter whether I talk quietly or scream; they do not hear. If I nudge them, they do not move. That's how I should react to sin. Temptation comes into my life and nudges me; I won't respond. Temptation may even try to argue with me or scream to get my attention. I do not respond—I am dead to it!

But what about the times when you haven't resisted temptation? You may feel you have made too many mistakes to be an example to others. You may think, *It's too late to make a difference.* If that were true, then no one, including me, would ever write a Christian book. But God can overcome any obstacle when we have a yielded, willing heart.

Wilma Rudolph, a world-renowned runner, almost didn't make it to the track. She was born into a poor black Southern family, the twentieth of twenty-two children. When Wilma was four years old she was diagnosed with polio. Doctors told Wilma's Bible-believing mother that Wilma would probably never walk again. But Mrs. Rudolph didn't think that was God's will for her little girl! She never gave up hope, and she worked tirelessly to help Wilma not only walk but run.

Wilma clung to her mother's faith. For over six years she had to wear a cumbersome brace, until one Sunday morning in church she took off her brace and walked down the aisle unassisted. She went on to become an excellent runner. At sixteen she captured a spot on the Olympic team. Although did not live up to her own expectations and captured only a bronze medal in the women's 400-meter relay, her coach still had high hopes for her future.

The next year Wilma started dating a young man. During a routine physical, she found out that she was pregnant. She was shocked. She had been too reserved to ask about sexuality, and her mother had been too reserved to tell her. This dilemma was hard on Wilma. She had embraced Christianity, and she felt she had disappointed not only God but her supportive parents as well. Her running coach at Tennessee State set aside a personal rule about not allowing mothers to train on his team. "The people I loved were sticking by me, and that alone took a lot of pressure, pain and guilt off my shoulders," said Wilma. She gave up social life in order to mother her baby. She disciplined herself to balance her running, her studies and her parenting.

Wilma secured a spot on the 1960 Olympic track and field team and sprinted into the history books as the first female to capture three gold medals. Her persistence had a snowball effect. Her wel-come-home parade was the first racially integrated event in her hometown's history. She opened once closed doors for other women athletes. And she later traveled with the Billy Graham team.

If you fall, don't say, "Oh, well" and use it as an excuse to continue sinning. Just agree with God that it was sin, and go on with the new plan of obedience to God. One mistake doesn't mean you'll never get it right. When children learn to walk, they fall down, but they keep on walking. No toddler says, "Well, I fell, so I'm just going to sit here for the rest of my life. It must be God's will." Success is just getting up one more time after a fall.

WHAT'S THE STANDARD?

When my husband and I built our home, I helped run the plumb lines. I would hold the top of the string and drop the weight down to see if the wall was square. Bill meticulously made sure we did it right. One evening I was tired and bored and said so. Bill reminded me that if we did this step wrong, the entire house would be unstable, and no amount of paint or decorating could make up for its structural weakness.

God's Word is the plumb line for our lives. If we measure ourselves by the standards of those around us, we will be only as good as the company we keep. God has planned something much better for us! Our attitudes, appearance and actions should be based on God's best for our lives. Our professional, ministry and volunteer work should be done well because we are doing it for God. Our parenting and friendships will be strengthened as we treat others as God would treat them.

INTEGRITY IS A JOURNEY

Sometimes we want to walk with Christ and be our best for him, but old habits nag at us. How can we ditch the old and put on the new self? How can we become comfortable with a holy lifestyle? Here are three steps I have found helpful.

Choose your focus. After my third son was born, I had to come home to an apartment in the center of a blasting site. A new development was going up next door, and the workers were blowing up the entire mountain to do it. It was mid-August, humid and hot, so we had all the windows open. The noise was horribly loud. My mother and I couldn't even carry on a conversation. To get any peace, I had to shut all the windows.

Similar chaos can threaten our spiritual lives. We are bombarded with lies from the media, society and our own sin nature—lies about ourselves, others and God. Satan is like a roaring lion whose his goal is to eat us alive (1 Peter 5:8). But we can shut the windows on the noise. The Bible tells us to take rebellious thoughts captive (2 Corinthians 10:5). When you fill your mind with the truth, you close off the lies.

Often when we come to Jesus and try to break bad habits, we focus only on the old. We tell ourselves, *Don't smoke. See that cigarette—don't smoke it.* Soon we are so consumed with *not* doing something that "it" is all we think about. Because "it" fills our thoughts, we wind up doing the exact thing we don't want to do!

Instead of focusing on what you are *not* going to do, decide what you *are going to do* in its place. If you don't want to overeat, choose an activity to replace eating at the times you usually fall. If you don't want to drink, don't go to the bar; go to AA or to a friend's home. If you don't want to spend money, don't go to the mall; go for a walk. If you don't want anything to control you, get a plan! Often the external sins are a symptom of an internal problem. You want a plan to address the internal hurt as well as the external behavior. If you have an escape plan ready ahead of time, you will be able to cope under pressure.

Change your "pink slip." When you purchase a used car, you get a pink slip that proves your ownership of the car. When Jesus came into your life, you gave him the pink slip to your heart. He's the new owner. You need to choose to read his owner's manual and run your life according to it.

Learning to follow Christ is easier with help. A trusted friend, counselor or pastor can be God's instrument to help you succeed in your choice to listen to God's voice. Someone who understands the principles of spiritual warfare can help you learn to respond to God.

Hang on to the lifeline. Commit yourself to a loving body of believers. After you take the first big step in healthy living and get grounded in the basics, you may be tempted to run away to a different group of believers who don't know you so well. Accountability can hurt. A wise woman of influence will invite input from godly people. Ask those you respect, "Is there anything in my life that keeps me from being all God designed me to be?" If God calls you to be the one to answer that question for someone else, know that sometimes people don't want to hear the truth! We may lose a relationship, maybe for a short time, maybe forever. But more often the other person will listen to us—listen to God's Word and God's love through us—and we will win a friend and gain her gratitude.

WHEN INFLUENCE ISN'T WANTED

Sarah approached me in panic. She was single and had just found out that she was pregnant. She had been on one of our youth leadership teams, but she had a weakness where men were concerned. Now the consequences of falling for a jerk had put her life in turmoil. Would I disciple her and help her out of this mess? I walked Sarah through telling her family about the pregnancy. Shortly afterward, when she miscarried, I went through it with her. In the months that followed, she grew and began to make healthy lifestyle decisions. Then suddenly she began to miss appointments and not finish her assignments. I discovered she was living with another man in a sexual relationship—the very thing she had wanted help not to do.

My stomach drew into a knot, but I knew I had to confront the situation. I shared my heart with Sarah. She saw that what she was doing was wrong, but she didn't want to give it up. She said she still wanted to meet with me and do Bible studies, and she was still interested in leadership someday. I had to explain that I would love to help her grow, but I couldn't help her grow if she refused to listen to advice that she knew was true. If I was to continue meeting with her, she would have to give up sex with her non-Christian boyfriend. Sarah said she would rather have her boyfriend than Jesus and walked out. I cried for her. I had tried to love her and support her. I had made it my goal to be compassionate, not judgmental. She had asked for my influence, and now she didn't want it. My prayer became, *God, she can walk away from me, but don't let her walk away from you.*

MAJOR IN MERCY

Years ago I began to pray for God's covering of grace and mercy over my life. Grace is God giving us what we do not deserve (salvation). Mercy is God not giving us what we do deserve (punishment for sin). Mercy and grace do not change God's character. Instead, the knowledge of his grace and mercy fully convinces me of God's love. As I meditate on God's grace and mercy and his great sacrifice that attained it for me on the cross, I am overwhelmed by his love. Obedience to God's Word becomes a natural choice based on my love relationship with him. Then I am motivated to pray, "God, don't just forgive my sin; keep me from sinning."

> *God, don't just forgive my sin; keep me from sinning.*

AGREE WITH JESUS

"Do you not know that your body is a temple of the Holy Spirit, who is in you, whom you have received from God? You are not your own; you were bought at a price. Therefore honor God with your body" (1 Corinthians 6:19-20). When I keep in mind that the Holy Spirit lives in me, I am often compelled to speak out. I've talked to convenience store owners about their porno racks. I've mentioned to video store owners why I do or do not shop at their establishments. I have been known to take my business elsewhere instead of having my car tuned up in a garage with a *Playboy* calendar on the wall. In the same way, if someone acts in a way that honors the Holy Spirit within me, I affirm that person. When an employee is particularly helpful, I write a note to the head office. I explain to a business owner why I am a regular customer. I drop the Christian lingo, but somehow I refer to God, or I sign the letter with "God bless" or a verse of Scripture.

Sometimes I don't speak—I just react. When my son Zach was little, we were eating lunch at McDonald's when a massive man and his buddies sat down in the booth behind us. They promptly started talking, loudly, and the air whirled blue with obscenities. Zach leaned over and said, "Mom, can we move? Jesus inside me doesn't like those words." Because Jesus inside me agreed, we moved.

I also need to agree with Jesus when he shows me that my words or actions are wrong. One day I was at the home of a new friend. As we talked about life and ministry, our conversation slipped into discussing someone's life over which we had no influence. As I walked home, the Holy Spirit convicted me of my sin of gossip. I tried to rationalize it. *God, I'm a leader. I can't apologize to my new friend for something this petty. She might lose respect for me. God, what if I do apologize and she feels I'm judging her? She might not want to be my friend, and I really want her to be my friend. Really, Lord, it wasn't that big of a deal— we were just sharing our convictions.* But as I walked along, I knew I had to call her as soon as I got home, and I had to leave the results to God.

"Jenna, I just had to call and tell you I'm sorry for the things I said about Margaret. It wasn't my place to say them, and I am sorry for dragging you into the conversation."

"Pam, I'm so glad you called. I was feeling the same way, and I was just standing here trying to decide whether I should call you." Our friendship was cemented that day because I agreed with Jesus.

THE SIN OF PRIDE

One of the ugliest sins I ever had to confront was my own pride. Everywhere I turned, God was pointing out pride. All the illustrations I heard in sermons, all the topics at a conference I attended, all the conversations with other women of influence centered around pride.

I caught myself wondering how I could be guilty of pride, since so often I battle a self-confidence problem. Then God pointed out that oversensitive low self-esteem is pride inside out. When I battle low self-esteem, I am still focusing on me. I am concentrating on seeking approval and encouragement. My eyes are on my needs, while God wants my eyes on him.

During that time, God brought to my mind all the ugly words that I had never voiced but had thought. *Why is she so rich when I have just as much talent? Why is she teaching when I know as much as she does? Why is God blessing that ministry with huge numbers instead of ours?* In my complaints I was telling God that his plan was wrong and mine was right. Pride made me play God in my own life. My heart was broken over my sin. I got away to a private place with God; I fell to my knees and wept. I listed every good thing, every compliment I could remember, and I thanked God for what he had accomplished through me, or rather in spite of me.

God's grace brought my pride to the surface to be skimmed off.

When goldsmiths create pure gold, they heat up the fire, and the dross and impurities come to the surface. The goldsmiths skim off the impurities until they can see their own reflection in the gold. God's grace brought my pride to the surface to be skimmed off. I wanted the impurities taken out of my life until people could see God in me.

Afterward I wanted to keep my confession between God and myself, but God stoked up the fire again. I felt that he wanted me to openly confess my hidden sin of pride. I was afraid of the criticism my confession would bring on me. After all, I was a leader. I should have dealt with pride long ago. God showed me when he wanted me to confess and to whom.

I was discipling a small group of women leaders, and I shared my confession and restoration with them. Later on a Sunday night I stood up in front of our congregation during a sharing time and told the highlights of what I had learned from God. I knew then I was free, because I didn't care if they thought less of me; God had accepted me by his grace. My slate was clean. I did hear some criticism through the grapevine, but mostly I felt personal relief for a burden laid down. And there was another benefit: a new transparency developed in those who were following my leadership. Because I was honest enough to expose the ugliness of my sin, others felt free to ask for help with hidden areas they had battled for years.

Sometimes I choose to rein in my freedom for the sake of another.

HARNESS YOUR FREEDOM

A policewoman in the bomb division wore a shirt that identified her as a "Hazardous Device Technician." The back of her shirt read, "If you see me running, try to keep up!" That should be our motto. People should see us running away from sin and running to righteousness, and they should feel compelled to follow. Paul advised the Corinthians to follow him as he followed Christ (1 Corinthians 11:1). People should be able to follow in our footsteps as we seek to walk in the footsteps of Jesus.

My mother used to say, "When in doubt, don't." Scripture puts it this way: "'Everything is permissible for me'—but not everything is beneficial" (1 Corinthians 6:12). If I am free to do something, that doesn't mean I am compelled to do it. Sometimes I choose to rein in my freedom for the sake of another.

While I was in junior college, disco dancing was the rage. I loved to dance, and I was good at it. But one night it all changed. I went to a nonalcoholic teen club where I danced every dance. My plan was that during the break and during slow dances, I would share my testimony with the men I danced with. Then a young man whispered some very obscene things he wanted to do with me after we finished dancing.

I was shocked. I felt confused, guilty, dirty and angry. My heart was pure, but my body had given out an entirely different message! I felt like I had really let Jesus down and that the words *tease* and *fake* were tattooed on my forehead. I wanted to scream, "Don't you all understand? I really do love Jesus! I didn't mean to be seductive! I want you to know my Jesus—but you can't, I'm standing in your way!" That was my last night at the disco. If that type of dancing caused such confusion, I would give up that style. I would give up anything that hindered others from coming to Christ. Other people's spiritual lives became more important than my rights.

Other people's spiritual lives are more important than our rights.

Like the apostle Paul, we want to be "all things to all people, that [we] might by all means save some" (1 Corinthians 9:22 NRSV). At the same time we want to be careful "that the exercise of [our] freedom does not become a stumbling block to the weak" (1 Corinthians 8:9). If we stray too far in one direction, we can become legalistic and set up barriers for people who are seeking Jesus. If we stray too far in the other direction, we may live no differently from those who are apart from Christ, and they may never see Jesus in us.

EMBRACING INTEGRITY

One of my favorite recent examples of a woman of integrity is Condoleezza Rice, Secretary of State under President George W. Bush. She is a woman of influence because her measuring rod is excellence rather than mediocrity. "Condi" is a pastor's daughter who grew up in Birmingham, Alabama, during the height of the civil rights movement. She says, "My parents had me absolutely convinced that . . . you may not be able to have a hamburger at Woolworth's but you can be president of the United States!" Her parents taught her that she had to be twice as good to gain equal footing and three times as good to surpass expectations. This inner voice helped Condi shatter nearly every glass ceiling placed before her. Her parents came from a long line of educators. To Condi's natural abilities they added such a strong work ethic and self-discipline that she skipped both first and seventh grade. She entered the University of Denver before age sixteen.

At first Condoleezza Rice studied to be a concert pianist. When she realized that she did not have the talent to play among the elite in concert halls, she shifted her energy to Russian studies, graduating cum laude at age nineteen. Her passion for Russia and for foreign policy took her into the halls of Stanford University as a professor, then as Stanford's youngest, first nonwhite and first female provost. At a dinner party Condi impressed Brent Scowcroft, later national security advisor. Scowcroft was instrumental in persuading Condi to set aside her teaching career to serve in the White House. Condi gained the title of national security advisor and then secretary of state.

Condoleezza Rice credits her faith in God as the driving force behind her strength of character. She says, "When I'm concerned about

Only time will tell how far God will elevate a woman who has dedicated herself to a lifestyle of serving with excellence.

something, I figure out a plan of action, and then I give it to God. I just ask to be carried through it. God's never failed me yet." Many people believe Condi has the résumé and integrity for the role of first female and first African American vice president or president of the United States. Only time will tell how far God will elevate a woman who has dedicated herself to a lifestyle of serving with excellence.

LIVING IT OUT

In what areas of your life is God leading you to repent or to make amends? In what areas do you want to raise your standard of excellence? Meet with a trusted friend, mentor or counselor and ask for encouragement for your journey.

How can you move from sin to restoration? God wants to move you from a broken place to a better place.

- *Acknowledge your sin.* Whether you call it your mistakes, failures, imperfections, bad attitudes or anything else, acknowledge it to God. "He who conceals his sins does not prosper, but whoever confesses and renounces them finds mercy" (Proverbs 28:13).

- *Accept God's grace.* "And the LORD said, "I will cause all my goodness to pass in front of you. . . . I will have mercy on whom I will have mercy, and I will have compassion on whom I will have compassion" (Exodus 33:19). God longs to extend his grace and mercy to you. He holds it out as a gift; simply reach out and take what he offers.

- *Amend your mistakes.* If you have hurt someone, apologize. If you can correct the wrong, offer to do so. Jesus said, "If you are offering your gift at the altar and there remember that your brother has something against you, leave your gift there in front of the altar. First go and be reconciled to your brother; then come and offer your gift" (Matthew 5:23-24). If you have a bad habit or bad attitude, replace it with a better choice or better attitude. Memorize Scripture to renew your mind so you think about yourself as God thinks.

- *Actively pursue accountability.* Ask a friend or mentor to help you learn new ways to overcome wrong patterns of thinking and acting.

8

INTENSE
Staying Power for the Long Haul

A woman is like a tea bag—

only in hot water do you realize how strong she is.

NANCY REAGAN

*I*t was a photo finish. Gail Devers and the other competitors in the hundred-meter dash walked and waited. The instant replay board in the Olympic stadium flashed the images of the four runners. The winner was still indiscernible.

Walking and waiting were activities Gail did not take for granted. Just over a year before this race, she had been waiting to hear if she would ever walk again.

In 1988 Gail set a U.S. record in the hundred-meter hurdles. Then a mysterious illness began to ravage her body. Her hair came out in handfuls. Her world went from cloudy to dark as she lost most of her eyesight. Her body shrank as she lost over forty pounds. She lost large amounts of blood. "My feet were swollen and oozing yellow fluid," she says. "I had little holes all over my feet." Unable to cope, her husband left her. Because Gail's feet could no longer bear her weight, her parents moved in with her to care for her. It was humiliating to accept help for even the most basic needs like being carried to the bathroom.

In March 1991 Gail visited a new doctor who recognized her symptoms as a reaction to radiation treatments for Graves disease. Because she believed God would allow her to run in the Olympics, she had declined the traditional treatment for Graves, a beta blocker that was on the Olympic list of banned drugs. The medical staff was able to revise her treatment, and within a month she walked a lap around the UCLA track in socks—her first workout in two years.

"I felt I was washed up in track, that there was no way I could ever come back. . . . I was scared. I was just hoping God would save my feet so I would be able to walk again." But Gail prayed. Her pastor father prayed. Her mother and all her friends prayed. Her coach, Bob Kersee, prayed and believed that Gail would come back.

Gail started walking, then jogging, then running. One step at a time, literally, she came back. After each workout she had to cut off her socks and watch her skin peel off with the cotton. As her coach doctored her feet, he would keep telling her to keep going, keep believing, keep looking up.

As the Olympics neared, Gail still stayed clear of the medication that would have helped her Graves disease. She had pushed through the pain and agony, and she was going to steer clear of any drug controversy. On the day of the Olympic race, Gail's feet were broken out and she could not feel the pressure of her right foot in the starting block. But when the starter's gun fired, she instinctively shot into action.

The judges finally made their announcement. Gail had won the hundred-meter dash! Bob Kersee embraced his courageous competitor, looked her in the eyes and said, "You wanted it. You got it." Later

Gail told the press, "Use me as an example. When the walls are closing in, when someone doesn't know where to turn, tell people I was there. I kept going. So can others."

So can you—one step at a time.

THE STARTING BLOCKS

At a Christian conference center, during afternoon recreation time, I proposed an idea to a group of women. "See that mountain over there, and see that cross? I know how to get to the top. Does anyone want to go on an adventure? We could climb it—it only takes about an hour or two up and back." Four brave women stepped forward.

I confidently marched our little troop across the street and to the trailhead, or what I thought was the trailhead. We scaled up a brush trail only to come to a dead end. So we retreated. I assured my group, "I know the trail is marked with surveyor's ribbon. I really have been here before." I tried to instill confidence into myself as well as this band of women. Again we climbed to a dead end.

"How about this way?" one woman suggested.

"Try it!" I said. "And while you do that, I'll climb to the top of this rock and see if I can get a better perspective from up here."

This process went on for over an hour, all of us giving suggestions, taking turns leading, finding dead ends and then trying again. I wondered if my companions were starting to think it was all a waste of time. Surely we all weighed the option of bagging the whole idea and going to the store for chocolate. But after each try, we would make a new resolve. None of us wanted to quit.

Finally we all agreed on one last course of action—and sure enough, at the end of that trail was a very faded piece of red surveyor's ribbon. Now we could climb the mountain! We kept our eyes on the cross, our goal, and eventually we felt the cool refreshing breeze at the pinnacle of success.

Often it's at the beginning of a new venture that you encounter obstacles that scream *Go back!* What makes you want to quit before you get started? Is it the poorly marked trail ahead? Is it the steepness of the mountain? Is it the negative comments from friends or family? Or is it some hidden fear, deep in your own heart?

> *Too often, women quit too soon.*

Too often, women quit too soon. Sometimes the starting line is our quitting point! We want to be heroines but we don't want to act heroic. Success starts with the first step. It may take all your intensity just to get into the race!

WHAT IS INTENSITY?

The music is the moving ballad "Via Dolorosa," the story of Christ's walk to the cross. A beautiful young woman dances to the rhythm. She can't hear the music, but she feels its meaning. Heather Whitestone is deaf. This night she dances to victory and becomes Miss America.

Heather's road to victory began when she was a toddler. Her mom was determined to get her little girl off the sidelines and into the mainstream. She would stand with Heather and say a word. Heather was not allowed to run and play until she listened intently and said the right word. Heather went on to learn lip reading, then sign language. "Attitudes will handicap you more than anything in this world," she says. A poster of Heather wearing her crown sums it up: "They said she would only be able to get a third-grade education. Fortunately, she wasn't listening."

The road was intense, but Heather knew God wanted her to keep going. She says, "We are all worthy to Him." Heather hopes to encourage others to hang in there. "My crown should erase the word 'impossible' from their vocabulary."

Intense women perform diligently, earnestly and strenuously in order to reach a predetermined goal. When one of my boys was a baby, I sat in the rocker, nursing my little one and praying. This calm moment was a welcome relief from hectic circumstances. Life was coming at me fast, and I was not sure if I was ready. I turned on a tape. The speaker compared women to boats, saying some women are little rowboats that are easily capsized with only a bucket of adversity, while others are stronger and more stable. As I rocked, I prayed, *God, make me an aircraft carrier, where other women can come, refuel and be off again to accomplish the flight plan you have for them. Stretch me, fortify me, empower me through your power to be an aircraft carrier.* I was praying for intensity.

As I talk with business owners, managers, directors of volunteer organizations and church leaders, they all express the same desire: "We wish we could find people who will stick to the task." Businesswoman Mary Kay Ash says, "A person with commitment is worth one hundred with just an interest."

Susan B. Anthony was a woman who understood intensity. Susan was one of several women who were determined to secure women's right to vote. She also stood strong in the temperance movement and fought for the abolition of slavery.

As a child Susan learned the value of hard work. Her chores included baking twenty-one loaves of bread in a day. She learned teamwork side by side with local farm girls in her father's cotton mill. Often these girls were beaten by drunken husbands who used their wives' hard-earned wages for more liquor. Seeing the injustice, Susan was moved to take action. She became a schoolteacher, but her earnings were one-fifth of what her male colleagues received, so she protested. She persisted in visiting Negroes in their homes; she saw the visits as part of her role as a teacher in the community. Her actions brought disfavor, and she was fired.

Susan B. Anthony was made president of the Daughters for Temper-

ance. In 1852 she was barred from addressing a temperance convention because of her gender. God used the experience to shift Susan's focus, and she became a driving force behind the women's suffrage
movement. Teamed with Elizabeth Stanton, Susan tirelessly worked to
gain the vote for women. She traveled, spoke, researched and
marched. In 1872 she led a group of women to participate illegally in
a national election, to test the right of women to vote under the newly
adopted Fourteenth Amendment. She was
arrested, tried and fined for the act of civil
disobedience. She refused to pay the fine.
She declared to the judge, "Resistance to
tyranny is obedience to God."

The most important priorities aren't measured in minutes, hours or days but in multiplied years.

Susan B. Anthony never did cast a legal
ballot. Upon her death on March 13,
1906, only four states had granted
women the right to vote. However, four-
teen years later the Nineteenth Amendment was passed, and all women were
guaranteed the right to vote.

Susan B. Anthony was single-minded for over forty years. Many
women have difficulty sticking to a task for forty days! The most important priorities aren't measured in minutes, hours or days but in
multiplied years.

STAY IN THE RACE

How do we gain the intensity to endure? How do we put up with
pressure? How can we bear what life is requiring us to bear?

Jill Briscoe tells of visiting the killing fields of Cambodia. Her
translator was a small woman who had lost her mother, her father
and six brothers and sisters in the genocide. In this single killing
field was a towering monument filled with over nine thousand

skulls, including those of the interpreter's relatives. Jill groped for comforting words in the face of such tragedy. The Cambodian woman replied, "You in the West, when trouble comes, say, get this off my back, God. We in the East say, strengthen my back to bear it, God."

The power to stay in the race comes from God himself.

The power to stay in the race comes from God himself. When we undergo any trial, we should focus on the character and power of God rather than on the trial itself. The apostle Paul understood this when he wrote, "We have this treasure in jars of clay to show that this all-surpassing power is from God and not from us. We are hard pressed on every side, but not crushed; perplexed, but not in despair; persecuted, but not abandoned; struck down, but not destroyed. We always carry around in our body the death of Jesus, so that the life of Jesus may also be revealed in our body" (2 Corinthians 4:7-10).

A friend sent me a letter from Colombia shortly after someone on the same mission compound had been abducted by guerrillas. The letter said, "A few years ago a missionary was taken and later killed. Most feel that this current situation will blow over with time. I hope so. Even so, I feel that it's better to be where I believe God has led me and be at risk than to be safe somewhere else and out of God's will."

At the core of intensity is the ability to stay.

At the core of intensity is the ability to stay. "When you are tempted, he will also provide a way out so that you can stand up under it" (1 Corinthians 10:13). The word *abide* means "to pitch a tent." Intensity means that you pull out your hammer and pound in the stakes and move in— and stay until the task is accomplished or the circumstance is seen through. If we are in God's will, we have God's promise that he will help us "stand up under it" or he will "provide a way out" that maintains our integrity.

KEEP YOUR EYES ON THE FINISH LINE

I love to watch the hundred-meter dash. The competitors stretch and strain to propel every centimeter of their bodies forward. The finish is always dramatic as the runner pushes her chest forward, then throws open her arms as she breaks the tape.

At Calvary, Jesus kept the finish line in sight.

"Let us run with perseverance the race marked out for us. Let us fix our eyes on Jesus, the author and perfecter of our faith, who for the joy set before him endured the cross, scorning its shame, and sat down at the right hand of the throne of God" (Hebrews 12:1-2). At Calvary, Jesus kept the finish line in sight. We know that this earthly race has a wonderful and everlasting reward! Because we were worth it to Jesus and he ran the race for us, we can now race for him.

LISTEN TO THE COACH

Each year I help plan and facilitate our church's family camp. One year, camp came on the heels of months of hectic activity. On the last day of camp I woke up tired because God had kept me up most of the night dealing with my attitude. My heavenly Coach wanted to correct a harmful pattern in me.

I was overwhelmed with worry and anxiety for the camp. From all external signs it was going well. People were having a good time, new relationships were developing, significant conversations and decisions had taken place. Still I couldn't shake the feeling that I had to make everything work perfectly.

Writing in my journal, I realized my problem. As a child, my role in the family was to make things right. If my parents fought, I saw it as my job to reconcile them. If my brother or sister felt attacked or insecure, I took on the role of comforter. If Mom seemed shaken, I wanted to be her stability. I thought I had to be in control so chaos would not rule our home. I was allowing that old need to feel in control to creep back into my thinking. But God showed me again what I already knew to be true. Control was not my job. *He was in control!*

God has been working this soul-shattering character trait out of my life. Now when I feel burned out, I step to the side and listen for the voice of my Coach. God cares about you, your ministry, your family, your future. He will send you what you need to move forward in victory.

One day during a particularly difficult time of ministry, I received yet another hard, emotionally painful phone call. Soon afterward I had to pick up my son Caleb at the junior high. I had been crying, so I put on sunglasses in the hope that Caleb wouldn't see my teary eyes. However, he is a perceptive child. He asked, "What's wrong, mom?"

"It's a grownup issue, honey. Thanks for asking, but God will send an answer to Daddy and me."

"Oh, I know that, Mom. I'm reading this book by Charles Spurgeon about the Holy Spirit. God is all-knowing and he knows exactly what you need right now. He is all-powerful so he can go get exactly what you need. And he is all-loving so he is motivated to go get exactly what you need right now."

I smiled and looked at my precious son and said, "God already did—he sent you."

Whatever you are going through right now, God knows and he is motivated to move on your behalf.

COMBATING BURNOUT

Women of influence are women who give a lot to others, but we can't outgive God. When we're feeling burned out and on the verge of exhaustion, God has a plan to restore us.

In 1 Kings 18, the prophet Elijah accomplished one of the greatest victories of his life. The nation was gathered on top of Mount Carmel for a showdown between the false god Baal and the true God of Israel. There was a severe drought. The four hundred fifty prophets of Baal prayed to their god. They prayed all morning. Then they prayed and danced. Then they prayed and cut themselves. They prayed and tried their frantic prophesying. No response. The time for the evening offering rolled around, and still no Baal.

Elijah then took twelve stones, one for each tribe in Israel, and built an altar. He dug a trench around the altar, laid the offering on the altar and drenched the whole thing with water. Three times he drenched the sacrifice with water. Then Elijah prayed—once—and the fire of the Lord fell and burned up the sacrifice, the altar, the water and the soil! The people fell down and worshiped the true God, and the prophets of Baal ran for their lives. The prophets of God captured them and took them to the Kishon Valley and killed them.

Elijah was exhausted. He climbed back to the top of Mount Carmel, bent down to the ground and put his face between his knees. His day wasn't over! He was praying for rain! Seven times he sent his servant to check for rain clouds while he kept praying. Then it rained. Elijah urged King Ahab to return to the city in his chariot. "The power of the LORD came upon Elijah and, tucking his cloak into his belt, he ran ahead of Ahab all the way to Jezreel" (1 Kings 18:46). Jezreel was about twenty-five miles from Mount Carmel!

RESTORATION STEP 1: PRAY

When a responsibility ends, there are usually loose ends to take care of, but no one wants to do it because everyone is exhausted. We are tempted to stop short. Elijah may have felt that way. A drought was in the land; the people had repented, and so Elijah asked for rain. Not only did he get the needed rain, he got personally empowered for the next leg of his journey. What Elijah probably felt like doing was taking a nap, right there on top of the mountain! But he made a much wiser move: he prayed.

Sometimes I am near the end of a project, feeling sleep-deprived and brain-dead, with a deadline looming. Then I beg God for renewed strength. I climb in the shower and pray and sing praises. Ten minutes later, I feel like a new woman. I don't mean that I should make that practice a lifestyle. I cannot presume upon God's grace to cover for months and years of abuse to my body or mismanagement of my time or my spirit. But when I have been obedient and given my all, and I'm still coming up short of what it takes to complete a project and glorify God, God does make up the distance. Over and over again I have seen God's ability to swoop in and carry me to the finish line.

RESTORATION STEP 2: PREPARE FOR ATTACK

After you have accomplished something you know was only by God's power and grace, watch out for flying arrows! Satan wants to destroy your joy. He wants to make you ineffective or overly introspective so you associate negative emotions with doing great things with God.

Elijah's attack came from a crotchety, manipulative woman— Ahab's wife, Queen Jezebel. She was furious that her prophets were dead, and she wanted Elijah to pay. She put out a death threat on Elijah. Elijah, the man who had just witnessed the miraculous power of God, ran for his life! He sat under a tree and said, "I have had enough, LORD. . . . Take my life" (1 Kings 19:4).

If Satan can't distort your picture of God, he'll distort your view of yourself. Elijah's perspective was definitely off! We should never doubt in the darkness what we know to be true in the light.

Restoration Step 3: Put Your Feet Up!

Our first weekend in full-time ministry was unbelievably exhausting. My brother was getting married that Saturday. On Friday evening my family flew in and we decorated the church and hall for the wedding. Arriving at our new little apartment, we saw a throng of people—and most of our belongings flung across the lawn. My new little next-door neighbor, who was about four, came running up to me. "I saw water. It was a big flood! But I got Mr. Manager." I gave her a big hug and kept walking. A few relatives had arrived before us. Along with the manager, a carpet-cleaning team and my mother, they were trying to sort through the mess.

We had one hour to change clothes and be back at the church for the wedding rehearsal. Somehow everyone pitched in, and our wonderful Christian manager whisked us out the door and said he'd handle the rest. The wedding rehearsal and dinner lasted until late that evening. On Saturday we took care of last-minute wedding preparations, sorted through damp personal belongings, took part in the wedding, came home and cleaned up.

On Sunday morning at eight, Bill and I, holding six-month-old Brock, stood and smiled at the front of the church. Bill was being installed as the new youth pastor. Because the family was all present, we had also chosen that Sunday for Brock's baby dedication. Between the two services we also had Sunday school to run, and then we were off to a big family lunch before everyone left town to return home.

At six we were back for the evening service, then off to a big church staff dinner in honor of our senior pastor's wife. By the time dinner was served, Brock was fussy. Poor guy, he'd been so jostled all weekend that even nursing didn't calm him down. I sat quietly in a room, isolated from the party, trying to feed him so we could rejoin the staff that I didn't even know well yet. For forty minutes I tried twisting God's arm with my theology. *God, you control all things. Make*

Brock go to sleep! I finally gave up and took my crying baby to his daddy. Bill encouraged me to get something to eat.

Sometimes it's not a spiritual problem; you just need a nap!

Charlotte, the pastor's wife, met me at the table and asked me how I was. I broke down. In a rush I recounted the whole wonderful/terrible weekend, feeling guilty the entire time for crying at her birthday party. She lovingly put her arms around me and said, "Oh, honey, you're just tired. A long time ago, a wise woman in ministry told me that tiredness is Satan's tool. Sometimes it's not a spiritual problem; you just need a nap!"

Rest. We all need it. Rest includes adequate sleep, nutritious food, exercise and a slower pace of life. An angel of the Lord touched Elijah and said, "Get up and eat." There was water and fresh bread, straight from the heavenly oven. Elijah ate, then fell asleep again. Later the angel woke him again and urged him to eat to prepare for the next leg of his journey.

When we hit times of stress, often we grab what is quickest and easiest to eat. These foods are usually not the best nutritionally. Sometimes stress makes us forget to eat altogether. Stormie Omartian, in *Greater Health God's Way,* suggests a helpful guideline: eating pure food the way God made it. This simply means avoiding prepared foods and choosing foods that are closest to the way you would eat them if you grew them yourself.

Sometimes the best way to help our body and our spirit recover is to fast for a day or so, drinking water only, or maybe just clear juices and liquids. Fasting accompanied with prayer can renew the spirit as well as the body.

If you choose to eat in a healthier manner, don't fall into a legalistic attitude that says you are more spiritual because you have a certain diet. Good eating habits are important, but so are good attitudes. Elijah took what God gave him and ate it. Elijah didn't go on a crusade to change all of Israel's eating habits. He simply ate and rested in God.

Elijah had gained enough strength to travel forty days and forty nights to the mountain of God. This is the same place where Moses had heard God speak in the burning bush and where the Law had been given. Elijah returned to where he knew God had spoken. He needed God to speak to him again.

RESTORATION STEP 4: POUR IT OUT

God called to Elijah and asked him, "What are you doing here, Elijah?" (1 Kings 19:9). That question wasn't for God's benefit. He knew exactly what Elijah was doing facedown in a cave. God let Elijah dump. "I have been very zealous for the LORD God Almighty. The Israelites have rejected your covenant, broken down your altars, and put your prophets to death with the sword. I am the only one left, and now they are trying to kill me too" (1 Kings 19:10).

Well, Elijah had about half the story right. One woman was out to kill him. But he had run away from a revival, not a revolt. God told Elijah, "Go out and stand on the mountain in the presence of the LORD, for the LORD is about to pass by" (1 Kings 19:11). God told Elijah to get out of the dark, damp cave and stand up in the fresh air of the mountain where God would meet him. Often the most healthy thing we can do when we are depressed is get out of bed!

Elijah stepped out onto the mountain. "Then a great and powerful wind tore the mountains apart and shattered the rocks before the LORD, but the LORD was not in the wind. After the wind there was an earthquake, but the LORD was not in the earthquake. After the earthquake came a fire, but the LORD was not in the fire. And after the fire came a gentle whisper" (1 Kings 19:11-12).

When God wants to get our attention, things often get worse before they get better. Sometimes the wind, the earthquake and the fire are within our souls. God can use burnout to regain our attention. Sometimes he shakes the very foundations of our lives so we can see what we've been standing on. Sometimes his fire purges our heart of unhealthy thoughts, plans and desires. Sometimes he allows the wind to whip in and carry off anything in our life that is not nailed down. To really restore us, God will get us pared down to the necessary and the important. Then his gentle whisper will come.

God asked again, "What are you doing here, Elijah?" (1 Kings 19:13).

Elijah repeated the exact same answer as before. But God didn't accept it this time. He recommissioned Elijah and gave him a new mission. "Go back the way you came, and go to the Desert of Damascus. When you get there, anoint Hazael king over Aram. Also, anoint Jehu son of Nimshi king over Israel, and anoint Elisha son of Shaphat from Abel Meholah to succeed you as prophet. Jehu will put to death any who escape the sword of Hazael, and Elisha will put to death any who escape the sword of Jehu. Yet I reserve seven thousand in Israel—all whose knees have not bowed down to Baal and all whose mouths have not kissed him" (1 Kings 19:15-18).

Intensity is necessary for influence.

God restored Elijah's hope by reminding him of what was true: (1) You are called and needed. (2) I have a plan for your safety. (3) You are not alone. (4) Here is the network that will support you. Often when we are burned out, it is because we aren't believing one of those truths.

Intensity is necessary for influence. Intensity can accomplish what your heart can dream. What is stopping you short? What makes you give up on a plan? Why do you feel exhausted or discouraged? You can be an intense woman. Let God's gentle wind refresh your tired body and calm your frayed nerves.

Now turn your face to the Son and take a step—just one step—forward.

LIVING IT OUT

Which do you need today: to step up to the starting line, stay in the race, keep your eyes on the finish line, listen to your coach? What steps do you need to take to avoid burnout?

When I am really under the gun, I copy special verses and sayings that rekindle my strength, and I post them on bright-colored paper all over my home. Choose three or four sayings or verses, write them out and post them. Or go to bed with the Bible on CD playing in your ears. Choose a favorite verse, mail or e-mail it to a friend, and ask her to pray and believe God with you.

9

INQUIRING
Discovering How to Grow

When I stand before God at the end of my life,
I would hope that I would not have a single bit of talent left
and could say, "I used everything You gave me."

ERMA BOMBECK

*S*itting in a nursing home one day, Myrtie Howell prayed, *Lord, what more can I do for you? If you're ready for me, I'm ready to come. I want to die. Take me.*

Instead of taking her, God spoke clearly to her heart: *Write to prisoners.*

Myrtie said, "Lord, me write to prisoners? I ain't got no education, had to teach myself how to read and write. And I don't know nuthin' 'bout prisons."

She was right. At the time she hadn't heard of Prison Fellowship or any other Christian prison ministry. She wrote a letter and simply addressed it to the nearest prison she knew of: Atlanta Penitentiary,

Atlanta, Georgia. Myrtie went on to correspond with hundreds of inmates, sometimes as many as forty at one time.

When Chuck Colson went to visit this amazing woman, who was over ninety at the time, she told him, "So, now, Mr. Colson, you just keep remembering the Lord don't need no quitters."

Myrtie Howell shows us how each woman should move toward heaven: still stretching, still growing, still striving to reach upward and onward to God's glory. Many of us sink into our ruts and cover our heads, waiting for the heavenly trumpet to sound.

When a mother eagle constructs her home, she first lays down briars, jagged stones and all kinds of sharp objects that would seem unsuited for her purpose. She then covers this structure with a thick layer of wool, feathers and the fur of animals she has killed. She makes the nesting place soft and comfortable—a delightful sanctuary where she may hatch her young.

But the eaglets will not remain in their inviting cradle for long. The day comes when the mother stirs up the nest. With her sharp talons she tears away some of the soft, downy lining so her little ones will feel the sharp edges underneath. The young birds become so miserable that they are willing to get out and begin looking for their own food.

Change may make you feel as if your nest is being stolen right out from under you. If so, it's time for you to learn to fly!

LEARN THROUGH EXPERIENCE

My grandfather loves to remind me, "The best way to learn is by doing." A wise proverb says, "Experience is what you get when you don't get what you want. The school of hard knocks is an able teacher." Oscar Wilde said, "Experience is the one thing you can't get for nothing."

Experience showed me that I love to teach junior high, high school and college, but I'd rather someone else handled the preschoolers. Experience showed me that my heart was with women's issues rather than politics in general. Years of experience on the farm convinced me that I needed to go to college and major in English rather than agriculture. If running the farm had been up to me, I would have starved!

Experience helps us personalize what we do and gives us a methodology for doing it. Because I have taken in homeless people, I have a philosophy about the homeless. Because I've discipled scores of women, I have a discipleship method. Because I have worked with women in crisis year after year, I handle them differently than I did as a novice.

In my first few years in ministry, if someone called in a panic over her marriage, I felt I had to run right over and solve her problem. But I learned that if I always performed a rescue, the woman never learned to lean on God. She often did not finish taking steps to deal with the problem; she didn't need to, since I would fix things for her. If a problem has taken years to develop, it will probably take years (and lots of hard work) to be resolved. I now realize that I shouldn't work harder at a person's recovery than *she* is willing to work.

LEARN THROUGH A SMALL GROUP

It should be no surprise that small groups have revolutionized the church. Jesus sent out his disciples two by two. The whole group numbered only twelve at first. A small band of women also consistently followed Jesus. He promised, "Where two or three come together in my name, there am I with them" (Matthew 18:20).

Small groups can meet to study a specific topic, meet a specific need or accomplish a specific task. Small groups can be covenant groups with a goal of mutual accountability and growth. All a small group needs in order to get started is a leader—one person who gathers together one to a dozen other people. The reason and focus should be well established. Is this group primarily for Bible study? Is it primarily for encouragement or prayer? Is it primarily task-oriented? Are we gathered to facilitate a skill? How long will it run? Where will we meet? What roles need to be filled, and who will fill them?

Each year I challenge a group of women to become women of influence. These women share a similar vision for reaching the world, yet many lack training and a facilitator for their dreams. This is my favorite small group. We help each other stretch and grow in some very scary areas, and we become each other's stretcher-bearers in the midst of the battle. A member of one of the Women of Influence groups told me that she had grown more in one year in that group than she had grown in her previous thirty years as a believer.

I have a network of friends who are committed women of influence. Several of these friendships go all the way back to college, where I was in a small group with a handful of other women who were training for Christian leadership.

Grace was the friend who reconnected me with God. In college we swam on the same team and ministered side by side in Campus Crusade for Christ. She, her husband, my husband and I worked in youth ministry together. Her husband was the official youth pastor when we started, but the four of us grew to be a team. For a while Bill and I lived in an apartment directly over them. We were all newlyweds with no money but a huge commitment to Christ and a burning vision to see young people transformed for him. We ate together, prayed together, double-dated and ministered side by side. What set apart that relationship was our total honesty and transparency with each other. Transparency built week after week as we met together in a small group.

One day Grace, Steve, Bill and I were planning youth activities for the upcoming year. Steve wanted to take the youth group on a bike trip down the coast of California. I thought it was an outrageously crazy idea, and I spouted off my opinion in a very ungracious manner.

But Steve continued, "It'll be great! The motto can be 'Nothing's Too Tough to Make Me Complain!'"

We all agreed the kids needed to learn that lesson. Then I proceeded to complain about having to go on a bike trip! Finally the other three were able to get me reservedly on board, but I still had a bad attitude.

The next morning after Bible study, Grace asked me to stay for breakfast. She very lovingly confronted me about my attitude about the trip and the huge lack of respect I had shown. She calmly walked me through the episode and showed me how my words had stung. She was right. I was ashamed, but that conversation was a turning point in our relationship. Grace could lovingly confront—but just as lovingly, she continued to cheer me on, and still does today.

The bike trip turned out to be the adventure of a lifetime! On the back of every shirt was the trip's motto: *Nothing's Too Tough to Make Me Complain*. We had plenty of opportunities to practice putting our motto into action. The mountains were high and plentiful; the days were too hot and the seats too hard. My thighs burned; my back and arms ached from fatigue. One day our bike trailer came unhooked and several bikes (mine included) went over a cliff. But nothing was too tough to make us complain (much). Only bikes and clothes were lost—not people, not homes, not lives.

The lessons of the bike trip translated into deeper and more important challenges ahead. Most of the young people who took that trip are serving Christ today in some of the toughest ministry trenches. As women of influence, Grace and I continue to encourage one another up the steep hills of our lives.

LEARN THROUGH BEING MENTORED

Sometimes we need ongoing help with the process of growth. A discipleship relationship—where a more mature Christian woman *disci-ples,* or *mentors,* or *trains and encourages* a younger one in the faith—can be the lifeline we need. The goal of discipling is to present every woman complete in Christ so that she can win others to Christ, build others up spiritually and send them out in ministry—so that they in turn can win, build and send.

In the skilled trades, through the centuries, apprentices trained under master craftsmen to learn the intricate methods and secrets of producing exquisite masterpieces. As they worked side by side with the master, day after day, they caught much that was never formally taught. Mentoring works that way. Some of my most important insights have come from picking an older woman's brain. Over lunch or in some other one-on-one setting, I have the freedom to ask specific and often personal questions that wouldn't be covered in a large group.

There are many kinds of mentoring relationships. Some are short term and may last only a matter of days or weeks. Others are longer, enduring for years. This kind of honest relationship is a safe forum to sift out your thoughts, feelings, hopes, dreams, bad habits and stumbling blocks.

To start on this mentoring process, pray for God's guidance; then look around for possible mentors. Mentors may be busy people who will have to carve out time, or they may be retired and easily able to make time for you. You are looking for an older woman in the Lord. *Older* does not necessarily mean chronologically, but that she should be ahead of you in her spiritual journey with Christ.

Your mentor should be ahead of you in her spiritual journey with Christ.

As you prepare to begin learning from a mentor, ask yourself questions. What exactly do you want to learn from her? How much freedom will you give her to comment on what she observes in your life? Are you teachable enough to receive constructive criticism as well as praise?

Approach your potential mentor. Ask for a small amount of time at first, such as a lunch or a breakfast. Sometimes this initial contact will be all you achieve. The mentor may live too far away or have family or work responsibilities that don't allow her to be an ongoing part of your life. Still, much can be learned in a small amount of time. Some of my most treasured conversations have been in the form of letters or e-mails written to women whom I have respected and who have written back. Several times a mealtime conversation at a conference has profoundly influenced my ministry and career. Sometimes a certain phone conversation was exactly what I needed.

When you approach a potential mentor, be specific about what you want. Explain why you want to be discipled, why you'd like her to disciple you and what you'd like her to teach you. Ask if she would think and pray about it for a few days. Ask for a minimal amount of time at first—perhaps having lunch once a week for four to six weeks or getting together once a month for six months. If the time together proves valuable, then you can both agree to expand your mentoring relationship.

While my husband and I were at seminary, I formed two friendships that helped me learn the ropes of being a woman of influence.

Phoebe O'Neal was the wife of the dean of Talbot during our first year there. Phoebe challenged a few of us wives to leadership. We spent time, often over waffles, planning out a ministry to reach and equip student wives headed for ministry. But I learned much more from Phoebe. I learned how to keep a heart for a lost world; I learned how to be gracious and hospitable; I learned how to challenge in a way that was nonthreatening yet effective. In the many years since, I have learned from her example and her friendship. She is now a

widow with an entirely different role, yet she's still a woman of influence with a burning passion to reach her world.

My friendship with Sally Conway grew right after her first battle
with breast cancer. From Sally I learned how to keep first things first.
Sally had the ability to be perfectly composed when a storm raged
around her. People really mattered to Sally. She worked hard at helping me form my writing, but I was always more important to her than
my writing. Sally regarded me as a person, not a product.

I would drive all day to spend time with either Phoebe or Sally. After I spent time with them, I would always come away with a clearer
head and a bigger vision. They are older and have been through a lot
of what is still ahead for me, so when they said, "You'll get through
this," I actually believed it. When they said they'd pray for me, I knew
they did.

LEARN THROUGH BEING A MENTOR

When I met Tricia, she was a welfare mom living with a man outside
of marriage. She was shy and wounded, but I could tell she had a
heart of gold and an ability to trust God—when she knew what he
was saying to her.

One day, when I was driving her home, she asked if we could
meet from time to time. She wanted to know how to pray "right." I
was already praying about approaching her to see if she was interested in a discipleship relationship, and her request answered the
question. She had lots of questions about God, and we met week after week to answer them. One day I sensed she was ready to answer
one of my questions.

"Tricia, you know God really loves you—right?" She nodded her
head. "You know that he wants to give you a plan for your life that
will give you a future and a hope—right?" Again she nodded yes.
"Tricia, do you think it is God's best plan for you to keep living with

a man that you're not married to? Do you think it's God's plan for your kids?"

"You know, Pam, I've been thinking about that. What do you think?" Together we studied what the Bible said about marriage, commitment and God's ability to provide. Shortly afterward, I helped Tricia move out and get established in a new life.

Tricia eagerly learned God's principles, and she applied them no matter what the sacrifice. I encouraged her as she got into a job-training program; I helped her learn how to organize her home and her life; I cheered for her as she led many of her friends and family back to God. I applauded when she eventually married a godly man.

Tricia's oldest children are entering their teen years now, and they have wonderful hearts for God. Their mom has modeled simple and courageous faith in God, and it's passing on to the next generation. She has become a woman others go to when their lives are falling apart. She has also discovered a well of artistic talent, which God is using to reach and encourage others. I expect that Tricia and her children will continue to accomplish great things for God.

If you would like to be a discipler but no one has asked you, begin to pray regularly that God will bring you a younger Christian to whom you can give encouragement and teaching. Look around. If you sense that a certain woman needs discipling and is open to it, offer such a relationship on a short-term basis such as one hour a week for six weeks, and make it easy for her to decline if she wishes. Then see what God does through your relationship.

LEARN THROUGH LEADING

"A disciple is not above the teacher, but everyone who is fully qualified will be like the teacher" (Luke 6:40 NRSV). As you give your life away, women will grow more like you. And you will grow more like Jesus as you follow him. Having others following us keeps our hearts and minds attuned to God and motivates us to be going somewhere. The fact that women will be observing you, asking you questions and imitating your life can be intimidating—but it doesn't have to be paralyzing. Paul said, "Follow my example, as I follow the example of Christ" (1 Corinthians 11:1).

Most women don't see themselves as women of influence because they think they have to do some grand thing to be influential. In a relationship of influence, *being* is much more important than *doing*. I like to think of myself as a funnel. Jesus is funneling encouragement, information and guidance through me—but it's Jesus, not me, whom women follow.

Here are four ways to be what a younger Christian needs:

Jesus is funneling encouragement, information and guidance through me—but it's Jesus, not me, whom women follow.

- *Be prepared.* Let her see that you have vision for yourself and for her. Be prepared before your meetings, and expect the same of her. Provide her with extra resources as well as personal insights. Personalize your time with her to meet her needs, as you give her the basics to help her become a woman of influence.

- *Be transparent.* Share some of your struggles. Allow her to pray for you as you pray for her. Let her know you are not perfect, only obedient. If we aren't careful in this area, we give the false impression that only a chosen few can be women of influence. *Every* woman can influence.

- *Be available.* Open up your life. Let her see you in all kinds of life circumstances. Let her know when you are available and when you can't be reached. Let her know how to reach you in an emergency, then define *emergency*. You will be able to invest in only a few women in this way; let these few in closer to your life. Jesus spent extra time with three disciples, Peter, James and John. You can't influence everyone, but you can influence a few deeply.

• *Be challenging.* Don't be afraid to ask the hard questions. If the woman you're discipling isn't doing her assignments or taking the relationship seriously, talk to her about it. Explain that your time, her time and God's time are too precious to waste. Ask her if she thinks the expectations are realistic. If the relationship isn't working, God may be moving her on to someone who can better influence her; or he may want her to depend more on him and less on a person. Such snags are rare because a person who seeks out your advice and input is usually serious about growth; but if things get awkward, the best course is an honest conversation.

PASSING THE BATON

Passing the baton of influence to the next generation is an awesome blessing and a "perk" of obedience to God. It isn't always easy. Sometimes I tire of the hassle of rearranging my life to help others on their journey of growth. When I do, God reminds me that I once was a hassle.

I was an eighteen-year-old with lots of questions, lots of energy and no direction. Tina, the woman who discipled me in junior college, just about gave up on me on several occasions. She often had enough to do just to get me to date the right men and come to Bible study each week. I was a miserable failure at one of my first ministry jobs—making coffee and cleaning out the coffeepot.

One day, talking with Tina, I ran down the list of excuses why I couldn't keep a ministry commitment I had made. It was my birthday; my boyfriend was coming from out of town to take me out; he wasn't a Christian so he might feel uncomfortable at the Bible study; I had planned the date before I started discipleship. The list went on and on.

Finally Tina, grieved in her heart and tired of listening to my pathetic excuses, looked me straight in the eyes and with startling seriousness said, "Pam, who is more important to you, Jesus or your boyfriend?"

"Jesus," I replied.

And the Spirit inside me seemed to whisper to my heart, *Then why did she have to ask?*

For days I was upset. I took a long, hard look at my life. I kept my commitment. The calluses fell off my heart that day. It felt good to put Jesus first.

NATURAL GROWTH

On the Idaho farm where I grew up, there were two kinds of water. One kind was found in the many ponds that dotted the landscape. The ponds both fascinated and repelled us when we were children. They were filled with interesting insects and unusual plants. But because their water was stagnant, they were slimy with moss and sometimes smelled of disease and death. By sitting in the same place, the pond water had become no longer useful and even dangerous.

The other kind of water on our farm was the kind that ran freely. My favorite place to sit on hot summer days was on a wood-plank bridge over a narrow irrigation ditch in our back pasture. The water ran swift and cool. I'd dangle my feet in the flow and dream. I would drop a stick boat in the tiny river and watch it sail downstream. One day, as I dropped in my tiny boat, I thought of where that boat could go. It could float down the ditch and into the canal, down the canal and into the river, down the river and into the broad, blue ocean. I wanted to be on that tiny ship!

As we follow God and stretch and grow, you and I can sail beyond our horizon and out on God's boundless sea.

LIVING IT OUT

Right now you may need discipleship training that gives you a firm grasp of the basics of the Christian faith, or that deepens your roots in Christ, or that helps you overcome a weakness in your life. You may need training in how to reach out and help others grow. You may need mentoring—time with an older Christian who can help you grow in leadership skills, ministry or career. Or you may be ready to be a mentor and be stretched in the process. What is the next step in your growth?

Check the boxes below that you think will help expand your platform of Christian influence. Then meet a more mature woman for lunch and ask her what potential she sees in you that could be developed by following one of these steps.

☐ Take classes in _____.

☐ Get a degree in _____.

☐ Teach myself to _____.

☐ Learn about where God fits in my life by _____.

☐ Find someone to disciple me so I can grow. Ask _____.

☐ Find help in overcoming a particular weakness. Ask _____.

☐ Get professional counseling to deal with my troubled past. Call _____.

☐ Find a mentor. Possible women to ask: _____.

☐ Begin to mentor others. Possible women to approach: _____ _____.

☐ Join a small group. Call _____.

☐ Lead or begin a ministry that will equip others. Next step: _____.

10

INFECTIOUS
Being a Contagious Christian

Life is a coin. You can spend it any way you wish,
but you can spend it only once.

LILLIAN DICKSON

*T*here is no stopping a person who wholly belongs to God. The best gift God can receive is you—wholeheartedly, unreservedly you! God doesn't need your ability as much as your availability. If we are fired up for God, we will naturally influence others. Being fired up isn't just a state of mind. Being aflame for God is the overflow of a life plugged into God.

INFECTIOUS ATTITUDE

Karly asked me to disciple her during an especially busy time in my life. I did want to spend time with her because she reminded me of myself before someone made a space to disciple me. Since my schedule was already booked solid, I was honest with her. "The only way I can spend time with you is for you to just come along with me where

God doesn't need your ability as much as your availability.

I need to go." Karly agreed. So we have traveled together. Karly has cared for my children. We've folded my laundry, had meals together— and she has become like a daughter to me. If I had said, "No, I'm too busy," I would have missed one of the biggest blessings in my life. Karly has become a leader who mentors others. In college she founded a musical drama group, and each year she trains fifty or more kids to use music, movement and drama to reach out and share their faith. If you can't give all kinds of time, give the time you have. Just take younger women along with you as you serve God, and they will learn to serve God too.

TENACIOUS FLEXIBILITY

If you can't give all kinds of time, give the time you have.

Infectious women have a "can do" attitude. If you can get out of the house to meet a friend for lunch, you can do ministry. If you have half an hour for a phone chat with a friend, you can do ministry. If you have time for a hobby, you can do ministry. Yes, you may have to be more creative in the ministry obligations you commit to, but you can be a woman of influence.

One woman, married to an unbelieving husband, approached her pastor and asked to be allowed to meet with any woman who came to him for counsel concerning an unbelieving spouse. She loved her husband, but he allowed her only one hour of worship a week. However, she was free for ministry Monday through Friday during her lunch hour. She developed a lunch-hour mentoring ministry with other women like herself, encouraging them in their personal walks with God.

One day I exclaimed to her, "That must be so hard!"

She replied, "Sometimes it is. But I can't outgive God. He enriches me as I give to him. I won't use my circumstances for an excuse— God is bigger than that." Is there someone in circumstances similar to yours who needs to be encouraged?

Cynthia McKinney is a successful M.D. She is a vivacious African American Christian woman in the male-dominated world of medical science. Her patients love her. She is beautiful, talented and confident. When you meet her, you might think the obstacles she had to overcome were race, gender or economic issues. But, as for most women, Cynthia's biggest hurdle was her own lack of self-confidence.

Cynthia says, "I had to learn to believe God at his word and believe verses like Philippians 4:13 are true ["I can do everything through him who gives me strength"]. It was realizing that God always honors his Word. I had to take the Bible and make it personal. It is knowing the Lord is behind me and knowing that if I'm delighting myself in him, then he'll give me the desires of my heart."

You might think you don't have much to offer. Then offer God your prayers and your heart, and watch what he will do!

One weekend in 1990 a very small group of Texan teenagers came together. They had nothing to offer God except their passion and their broken hearts for their schools. They felt compelled to pray. That night they drove to three different schools. They didn't know exactly what to do, but they went to the school flagpoles and prayed for their friends, schools and leaders. The story spread to youth leaders across Texas. They got the idea that students throughout Texas would simultaneously meet at their school flagpoles to pray. At an early brainstorming session the challenge was named "See You at the Pole." The vision was shared with 20,000 students in June 1990 at Reunion Arena in Dallas, Texas. At 7:00 a.m. on September 12, 1990, in four different states, more than 45,000 teenagers met at school flagpoles to pray. A few months later at a national conference, youth pastors shared that their students had heard about the prayer movement in Texas and were equally burdened for their schools. On September 11, 1991, at 7:00 a.m., one million students gathered at school flagpoles all over the United States! After thirteen years the movement is still going strong. In 2004 over 2 million teenagers met for "See You at the Pole" across the nation and in countries as far away as Germany, Romania, South Korea, Japan, Congo and South Africa. The movement began with a handful of young people in an obscure town in Texas, and it flourished because their hearts were aflame for God and they were willing to radically obey.

You might feel overwhelmed by your own life circumstances—for example, if you are the mother of preschoolers, especially if you have several in diapers at once. One day a group of eight moms in a church, frantic to cope, got together in the home of one of the women. As they talked, they realized that their need was common to women, and for the next few years they stuck together and worked out a format that has exploded into MOPS (Mothers of Preschoolers). Now there are nearly 4,000 MOPS groups worldwide.

Do you feel too stressed to change the world? Maybe you have just one friend who needs a call from you.

Shirley is a woman who won't let her disease beat her. Diagnosed with multiple sclerosis, Shirley went from an athletic and active life— she was a piano teacher and Bible teacher—to lying in bed with the use of only her right hand and her mouth. For a time she continued to teach Bible studies in homes with the use of a specially designed car. When her body no longer allowed that, she became a phone counselor for a TV ministry. When her voice grew weak, she took to writing hundreds of notes of encouragement every month. Do you feel you can't do what you used to? Maybe you can't do it all, but what *can* you do?

Some women wonder why they should launch a new ministry

when there are already so many in existence. That didn't stop Lysa TerKeurst, who was challenged when she read Proverbs 31. She was stirred by the timeless teachings of a mother to her son explaining the kind of wife he should look for. Lysa wanted to offer the same message to women today. Proverbs 31 Ministries now has a radio program on over 1,000 stations, a magazine reaching nearly 6,000 women per month, a daily e-mail devotional with over 75,000 subscribers and online small groups through the website Crosswalk.com. Every generation needs women to carry the torch of truth to their peers. Will you carry the torch and help reignite your generation?

Will you carry the torch and help reignite your generation?

SOMETHING TO CELEBRATE

People like to be part of a winning team. As believers, we *are* a winning team. If anyone has something to sing about, if anyone has reason to tap their toes or cheer—*we* do. Celebrations are contagious.

We should look for reasons to celebrate—a raise, a promotion, an A on a paper, even a good hair day. Our family has adopted the tradition of throwing an "Angel Party" when someone comes to Christ. The idea comes from Luke 15:10 where Jesus says that the angels rejoice over one person's conversion. The angels have a party!

When I was in junior college, I started to notice how enthusiasm for life spreads to others. One morning at six, I carried my breakfast tray through the cafeteria line as I'd done all year. As usual, I greeted the workers. One of them said, "You are always smiling! What makes you so happy at this time of the morning?" God had given me one of my first "silver platter" opportunities to share my faith.

I said, "You really want to know?"

"Sure," was the reply.

"I know Jesus personally, so I am confident that today will be a good day, no matter what happens."

That scene has repeated itself over and over again.

Several families have come to Christ as a result of our friendships with them. Many of them are amazed that we act like normal human beings: we tell jokes, laugh, go to ball games, enjoy movies and barbecues and life. Bill and I pen books on relationships that teach truth with a humorous twist. You can tell by the titles: *Men Are Like Waffles, Women Are Like Spaghetti; Red Hot Monogamy; Every Marriage Is a Fixer Upper; Love, Honor and Forgive.* When prebelievers read our work, they often say things like, "It was so funny—yet so true! I didn't think Christians could make me laugh!" or "Wow, I didn't think married Christians *had* much sex, let alone *enjoyed* it! You mean God cares about all aspects of my life?" When our non-Christian friends are honest with us, they'll say, "You guys are real—and you're fun." Jesus brought joy, and so can we!

If all you do is spread hope, you will gain a growing circle of influence.

God has entrusted us with the gift of hope. You hold out hope by your smile, your laugh, your positive outlook on life and your ability to love. If all you do is spread hope, you will gain a growing circle of influence.

INFECTIOUS HOME

My children have benefited from our open-home policy. They have watched godly dating relationships develop. Over Sunday dinner, they have heard men and women speak of God's calling on their lives. They have also seen the ugly consequences of sin. They have come to hate alcoholism, drug abuse, abortion and domestic violence because they have seen what happens to the victims. I cannot fully shelter my boys from the pain of sin, nor do I want to. However, I am careful to maintain their personal privacy. Even when you are committed to being a woman of influence, your children shouldn't pay the price for your commitment. Give them the opportunity to buy into ministry at their own level of commitment, as they are ready.

When our son Brock was ten, he received a new bicycle as a community leadership award because several times he had voluntarily given up his own bedroom to help homeless young people trying to get a new start. What the newspeople didn't know is that Brock has given up his room all his life—for students in transition, missionaries on furlough and battered women. Each time we explain to Brock that it is optional for him to lend out his room for a day or so (once for several months). Each time Brock has responded with, "Sure—seems the least I can do." Years later Brock was named San Diego Citizen of the Year. He received college scholarships and was asked to address an audience of nearly 1,000. Even better, his servant heart drew his future wife to him. In her wedding vows she complimented him on his integrity and his respect for women and the gifts of women.

Give your children the opportunity to buy into ministry at their own level of commitment.

INFECTIOUS PURPOSE

Influence is a relationship with a purpose. If you can be a friend, you can influence.

Brenda, one of the first high school students I ever discipled, has shared Christ with far more women than I have, and she will continue to do so. Brenda is now a mother who leads women's ministry. Because mentoring is a conviction and a lifestyle for her, she is always discipling someone.

If you can be a friend, you can influence.

Brenda grew up in a solid Christian home. When she was a junior in high school, I challenged a small group of girls, including Brenda, to form a discipleship group. For over three years I spent time with these young women, pouring into their lives all I knew of God and training them to pass on the basics to others and influence their world. Years later Brenda said, "It was this training, the *whys* of Christianity, that stuck with me and became a basis for my life."

One day after a speaking engagement, a young woman came up to me and said, "You don't know me, but I feel I know you. See, I was discipled by Sheri, who was discipled by Kristin, who was discipled by Brenda, who was discipled by you—"

And I continued, "I was discipled by Tina, who was discipled by Faith, who was discipled by some awesome woman I am sure!" We could easily name six "generations" of discipling relationships!

INFECTIOUS LIFESTYLE

We are not meant to reach out only to younger believers. We can make contact with non-Christian women as well and be part of God's means of bringing them to faith.

Many Christians run from the world, fearing contamination. But the "contaminant" the world needs is the truth of the gospel, and we are the ones to spread it. We have a contagious hope, a contagious strength, a contagious joy. We need to run into the world. The world desperately needs to rub shoulders with us. Our lives need to be open to others as we work in retail, business, entertainment, education, science, medicine, media or ministry.

The world desperately needs to rub shoulders with us.

It's not as hard as you may think. To be effective in reaching and influencing a woman who doesn't know Christ, you need only do three simple things:

1. Meet her.

2. Answer her questions.

3. Be available to her.

MEET HER

Some of us don't influence the world around us because we aren't out in it. We may attend only Christian functions. We may work for Christian companies and organizations. We may have only Christian friends. We must get out of our safe Christian environment and simply meet people.

I look for strategic ways to alter my schedule to allow more non-Christians into my life.

If you came to Christ from a gang or drug culture, you may be afraid to go back lest you fall into the old temptations. That is a valid precaution, but it doesn't have to stop you from ministering. There are outreach groups that minister to people in neutral settings such as gyms, food and clothing distribution sites, or educational opportunities. You can meet new people at the park, at the laundromat, in volunteer work, in hobby groups and through your children's sports or other activities.

I look for strategic ways to alter my schedule to allow more non-Christians into my life. I enjoy aerobics, but instead of going to a church-sponsored class where most of the women are believers, I go to a secular gym. I already love to entertain, so instead of inviting just Christian people, I will carefully mix a party or invite all unbelievers. As my life changes with new obligations and responsibilities, I am careful to maintain a balance of influencing the world and influencing believers.

Jo-Anne Cinanni personally led more than forty friends to Christ in a six-year period. Jo-Anne met most of her friends through her second job at a diet and nutrition center where she works eight hours a week. Her life depicted the motto "Preach Jesus. If necessary, use words." Jo-Anne is convinced that words are a natural outflow of a heart connected to Christ. She says, "Jesus illustrates how we are to step into the world, reach out to sinners, and relate to them through our hearts in order to minister to them and show them God's love."

ANSWER HER QUESTIONS

Perhaps you hesitate to get into a spiritual discussion with a non-Christian friend because you're afraid she will ask some difficult question about the Bible, and you won't be able to answer. The good news is that you don't have to know all the answers; you only need to be available so your friend feels she can ask. You can always respond, "Great question. Let me do some research and get back to you." Then follow through!

You don't have to know all the answers; you only need to be available so your friend feels she can ask.

A bigger obstacle is the time it takes for a relationship to develop to the point of trust. It is too easy to keep things at a superficial level. It helps to have a good listening ear and ask a few well-chosen questions to get a friend talking. I don't want to sound like a quiz show host, but I do want to find out what she knows about Jesus and something of her personality, needs and desires. Does my new friend need intellectual answers to her skepticism, emotional answers for her heart or practical answers for her daily life?

In college, as a reentry student, I took a class in women's studies. The professor was a wonderful woman who encouraged free expression and debate. One day she walked in and started the class with a provocative question: "Today we are going to talk about when we first became sexually aware. Who wants to share first?" The class sat in nervous silence. Then I spoke up.

"Okay, I'll share," I said. I went on to explain how I came to Christ and that because of my trust in his love for me, I followed the guidelines in his book. I carefully chose my words so I shared my own experience but did not judge anyone else. I said that I had struggled with maintaining my virginity, but in retrospect I was glad. I explained that one benefit of that decision was the strong verbal communication that I now had with Bill. We can talk about anything, including sex, and as a result, we have a very enjoyable sex life.

An angry voice behind me interrupted, "You narrow-minded bigot! My mother tried to cram that religious crap down my throat, and now you're trying to do it too!"

Inside I panicked for a second. Then, because I feel securely loved by God and securely called to share him, I responded without defense and with grace. I turned toward the woman and apologized. I explained that I didn't mean to sound harsh. I only meant to explain what had worked for me. I smiled and my heart reached toward her, because she was obviously carrying around a lot of pain.

Hands shot up around the room. Other students, who I didn't even know were Christians, began to tell of their experiences. One young woman said that she had been sexually active with men but recently had come to Christ and was happier now, remaining pure and trusting God's plan for a future sexual relationship.

During the break I got to talk to many people about God and his love. After class I had a great heart-to-heart talk with my professor. My professor wondered if I was okay. I got to explain that I didn't feel my classmate had lashed out at me but at what I stood for. I shared my heart for women and men who have been hurt by legalistic religion, and I told of my spiritual journey. And my professor shared her own spiritual background and some of the questions she still had about God and Christianity.

In the classes that followed, I even had a few opportunities to talk with my classmate who had been so upset at me. I don't have all the answers, but I know what Jesus has done for me.

Because I believe so much in the power of the story, the women I mentor get an assignment to look for ten ways or ten words they can use as a springboard into their story of faith. For example, my ten words would be *marriage, love, dating, drinking, Dad, searching, parenting, children, college* and *perfectionism.* Any of these words can easily be a doorway into my life story.

The next assignment my disciples get is to try to tell their story without notes in a one-minute form, a three-minute form and a five-minute form, including a key theme and a key verse that sums up their story.

BE AVAILABLE

When we are prepared to tell our story, God gives us opportunities to do so. On the last day of class in Victorian Literature, we were discussing Joseph Conrad's *Heart of Darkness.* Earlier in the class I had shared some information on one of the passages from a Christian perspective. A young woman in the back of the classroom raised her hand and said, "It seems like those who claim to have a heart of light really have hearts of darkness, and those who are told they have dark hearts, like the natives, have enlightened hearts. It's just like Christian missionaries. They go into tribal cultures and push their 'gospel of light,' and it exploits the people."

Now some of my dearest friends work with tribal people on the mission field, and I know they aren't there exploiting the people. It is true that some horrible things have been done in the name of Christ; but for the most part, missionaries through the ages have brought native people health care, economic enrichment and hope.

Some tribal customs do change when the tribes come to belief in Christ. In the tribe where my close friends work, the tribespeople had the custom of hanging girl babies out in the forest for animals to kill. The practice developed because of their dowry system. The parents of the bride had to arrange a marriage and pay an often expensive and elaborate dowry. Many parents could not meet such an obligation, so instead of having to face it when their newborn girl grew up, they carried her into the jungle and left her hanging in a tree for wild animals to devour. As a consequence there is now a severe shortage of grown women in that tribe. Many men long for a wife and family, yet there are not enough women. But because many in the tribe have come to Christ, young girls' giggles again echo in the rain forest, instead of their desperate cries for help.

When we are prepared to tell our story, God gives us opportunities to do so.

All these things and more were buzzing in my head as I sat there in class. My heart was pounding as I tried to gather my thoughts and raise my hand.

Just then the professor said, "Good point. With that comment we will conclude our class. Thank you for attending. It has been nice having such a bright class. Have a nice summer."

Good point? Have a nice summer? That was not a good point! I can't

have a nice summer when this class ended in such darkness! Oh God, I let
you down!

I gathered my composure through prayer and thanked the professor for all his hard work, but before I got out of the classroom, tears were running down my face. *I'm so sorry, God! All semester I tried to represent you. Nearly every class, you gave me the opportunity to correct theology or make a point of logic. Now to have it end this way—it's too hard!*

I got in the car to drive to a creative writing class that I was to teach. I was crying so hard that I could barely see the road. I felt brokenhearted over my inability to find the words I needed. Then God reminded me of a promise: "Do not worry about what to say or how to say it. At that time you will be given what to say" (Matthew 10:19).

All semester God had given me the words. All semester God had given me the opportunity. That particular day, God had given me neither. I was available, but God did not choose to use me. Using me was God's responsibility. Being available was my responsibility. A sense of freedom flooded me. I held tight to that feeling. I also held tight to the utter brokenheartedness that I was experiencing. I do not want to ever forget either of those feelings.

NOW IS THE TIME

When Jesus left this world, he gave the Great Commission: "All authority in heaven and on earth has been given to me. Therefore go and make disciples of all nations, baptizing them in the name of the Father and of the Son and of the Holy Spirit, and teaching them to obey everything I have commanded you. And surely I am with you always, to the very end of the age" (Matthew 28:18-20). Jesus didn't say that only pastors or only directors of women's ministries or only executives should make disciples. His command is for every person who knows Jesus Christ personally.

You might be asking, "Where are the ordinary women? This book is full of extraordinary examples—what about me?" We are *all* ordinary, but God is extraordinary! Every Christian woman is to be a woman of influence. Every woman is to make disciples. Every woman is to go into the world and make a difference for Jesus. Whatever your gifts are, use them. Whatever your platform or position or experience, use it.

Don't wait for women to ask you to mentor them; challenge women to be mentored. Don't wait for a woman to challenge you to be mentored; ask her to mentor you. Don't wait until women in the world ask you for help; offer it ahead of time. Don't wait until they ask about Jesus; go tell them.

> *We are all ordinary, but God is extraordinary!*

NO EXCUSES!

If you have tried to be a woman of influence, you know it is a struggle. People have problems. Problems are a hassle. Sometimes it is inconvenient to care. We may not want the troubles that influence brings.

Kay Cole James went on television representing a local prolife effort in a late-night debate. Cards and letters poured into the National Right to Life office lauding her abilities. The leaders of National Right to Life came to her house, watched the tape of the debate and offered her a job on the spot. Kay turned them down. She was a successful businesswoman and mother, and she didn't want to further complicate her life.

A few months later Kay was listening to a tape in her car. An Episcopal priest gave a compelling call to involvement in the prolife movement. Kay describes her reaction: "It occurred to me that while this battle for the lives of millions of unborn children was going on around me, I could not hide myself behind a good job selling stereos and TV sets. Babies were dying because people like me didn't want to get involved."

Kay became the national spokesperson for the National Right to Life committee. She was so successful that soon Planned Parenthood representatives refused to debate her. She was a committed, articulate black woman with a passion.

Soon that passion caught the attention of the Republican party. One day she stopped by the Bush election campaign headquarters in Washington, D.C., to talk over some issues close to her heart. When George W. Bush heard she was there, he approached Kay and asked her to come on board with the new administration.

Kay stalled. She explained that her mother was ill with cancer and it just wasn't a good time. Then Kay went to visit her mother in the hospital. Kay shared the exciting offer and told her mother that she'd turned it down.

Her mother replied, "Girl, what's wrong with you! I raised you better than that! The son of the president of the United States asks you to serve your nation and you say no! How many people do you think get that opportunity? How many black folks you think being asked?! Girl, you bes' get back on that phone and tell him you was just kidding!"

Influence is worth the hassles because lives are changed for eternity. So what is stopping you from stepping out? To become women of influence, most women only need someone to believe in them. I believe in you—but most importantly, God believes in you!

MESSAGE IN MARBLE

I love traveling the northeastern United States. History comes alive in places like Boston, Lexington and Concord. One fall, while visiting the area, I walked into a graveyard next to a church. The day was crisp and blustery. I wandered through the cemetery, pushing the multicolored leaves away from the headstones and reading the words chiseled there. The personal qualities and major life achievements of the dead were etched in stone for all future generations to see. *This is what was important to her; this is what she lived for; this is who she lived for.*

What a privilege to be the artist, chisel in hand, tapping out tributes. The careful tapping of hammer against chisel created a permanent monument. These were not cold stone markers symbolizing death, but tributes memorializing life. I wondered, *God, at the end of my life, what will be etched in my stone?*

God moved within my heart: *Pam, you are writing your stone today. Write wisely.* I leaned back against a tree and, gazing at the nearest tombstone, tried to think of what God would chisel in the marble about my life:

Here lies Pamela Farrel . . . tap . . . tap . . . She believed God could do exceedingly abundantly beyond anything she could ask or think . . . tap . . . tap . . . She loved her husband, her children, her friends and relatives . . . She encouraged women to be all God created them to be.

Each day of life we chisel our influence into the hearts and lives of others. Christ is the artist. You are his tool. Only you can decide how you will allow the Master Craftsman to use your life. "One cannot transform a world except as individuals in the world are transformed, and individuals cannot be changed except as they are molded in the hands of the Master."

You and I must decide whom we are called to influence. Are our gifts and talents being used only for momentary popular recognition, or is our influence carving out influence for Christ for generations to come? Who are we living for: ourselves or the Master Craftsman who made us? You are a woman of influence . . . the Craftsman is working . . . tap . . . tap . . . to make a difference.

LIVING IT OUT

What do you want on your headstone? On the headstone below write three to five sentences that capture what's on your heart.

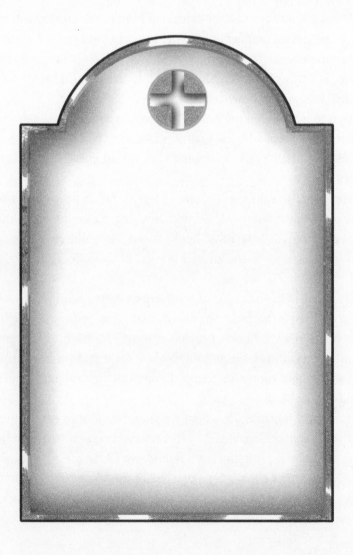

Bonus Section 1

LIVING IT EACH DAY
Twelve Weeks of Devotions

CHAPTER 1: IMPASSIONED

Day 1: Read Esther 4. What do you think transformed a quivering queen into a confident queen?

Brainstorm a list of ways to fill in the blank: "The world would be a better place if _____." What do your answers tell you about yourself?

Day 2: Read Luke 21:12-19.

Write down three or four times you were moved to tears or moved to take action, or both. What common threads do you see?

Day 3: Read Romans 8:28-39.

Interview a family member and a couple of close friends. What do they think you talk about the most? What do they think you are passionate about?

Day 4: Read John 14:23-27.

Examine the doctrinal statement of your church or some other statement of faith. Which truth(s) would you be willing to die for? go to jail for? Are there any tenets that you consider nonissues?

Day 5: Read Mark 13:9-13.

Write thank-you notes to women who have had a profound and positive effect on your life. Send them promptly!

Weekend: Read Jeremiah 1:4-8; Exodus 31:1-21.

Write about times you gave your life away—you were other-centered, you volunteered, you helped someone out in ministry and so forth. Look for patterns in what you write. Do you see any repeated types of people, repeated settings, repeated words such as *listened, taught, served,* etc.?

Consider any lifestyle or scheduling changes you need to make in order to step out into the passion or calling God has for you. Begin praying that God will align your heart and life with his will and calling for you. Make definite plans to make necessary changes.

CHAPTER 2: INDIVIDUAL

This week's Bible readings introduce various spiritual gifts that the Holy Spirit may exercise through your particular leadership style. As you read through them this week, place an asterisk by those abilities you think are your strongest.

Day 1: Read 1 Corinthians 12:1-6, 27-28; Romans 12:6-8. THE BOSS: Do you find joy in planning an activity, party or event to tell people about Jesus or to help people grow in their relationship with him? Possible gift: Leadership/Administration.

Read 2 Chronicles 2:5-10; Exodus 30:22-25. THE ARTIST: Do you like to use your craftsmanship to create something of beauty that can be used at church or in your home to remind people about God? Possible gift: Craftsmanship.

Read Romans 10:12-15; Ephesians 4:7-13. THE MEGAPHONE: Do

you feel the urge to talk to others about Jesus, share your story of faith or invite friends to church? Possible gift: Evangelist.

Day 2: Read 1 Corinthians 2:1-3; 12:8; Romans 12:8. THE COUNSELOR: Do you often find yourself listening to friends' problems, offering to pray with them or trying to find Scripture that will help them? Possible gifts: Exhortation or Wisdom.

Read Mark 12:41-44; Romans 12:8; 2 Corinthians 8:1-9. THE BANKER. Do you find joy in giving away money to help someone such as a missionary, a needy family, your church or some other ministry? Possible gift: Giving.

Read Mark 2:1-4; Romans 12:7; 16:1-2; 1 Corinthians 12:27-28. THE HELPER: Do you prefer to help behind the scenes, set up chairs, pass out fliers, make punch, pick up after Sunday school or youth group or do things a janitor or a secretary might do? Possible gift: Helps/Serving.

Day 3: Read Acts 16:11-15; Romans 12:9-13; 1 Peter 4:9-10. THE HOSTESS: Do you like to plan parties in your home, have overnight guests and make them feel comfortable, loan them your best things to use while they stay, make something and take it to a neighbor or an elderly person and stay and talk? Possible gift: Hospitality.

Read Acts 12:1-17; Philippians 1:19; Colossians 4:12; 1 Timothy 2:1-8. THE PRAYER WARRIOR: Would you willingly pray for one person for twenty minutes, pray out loud with someone who is sad or pray on your way to or from work or school? Possible gift: Intercession.

Read Romans 15:14; 1 Corinthians 12:8. THE BRAIN: Do you frequently offer to use your knowledge to help someone else, such as by tutoring, showing others how to do something or handling technical matters in your church office or sound system? Possible gift: Knowledge.

Day 4: Read Luke 10:30-37; Acts 16:29-34. THE NURSE: Do you find joy in helping those who are sick, disabled or older or weaker than you are, or those who need a boost such as special education children or children who need extra help in school? Possible gift: Mercy.

Read 1 Chronicles 16:39-42; 2 Chronicles 5:11-14. THE MUSI-CIAN: Do you jump at the chance to sing or play an instrument in church, at a nursing home, for youth group or for some other gathering, and would you like to write songs about God to play outside of church such as at school or a public event? Possible gift: Music.

Read Romans 12:7; 1 Corinthians 12:28; Ephesians 4:11; 2 Timothy 1:13-14; 2:1-2. THE TEACHER: Do you seek out opportunities to teach Bible studies in or out of church, teach your younger brothers and sisters, gather up kids in your neighborhood and teach them Bible stories, or volunteer in any way to help others learn about God? Possible gift: Teaching.

Read Psalm 45:1; Acts 15:19-20; 1 Timothy 3:14-15. THE WRITER: Do you prefer to use the written word rather than the spoken word to tell others about Jesus, whether through your own greeting cards, stories, poems, letters to the editor or other kinds of writing? Possible gift: Writing.

Day 5: Read Mark 10:35-45. Two of Jesus' disciples asked for special places of honor. Write what you learn about servant leadership from how Jesus dealt with their request.

Weekend: Read Luke 12:35-48. Leadership is a great joy and a great responsibility. What is the most encouraging thought about leadership that you received from chapter two of this book?

List all your leadership roles of the past. Which ones do you think were the most fruitful? Which were the most fulfilling? Ask God if this is a time to shift how you lead or whom you lead.

CHAPTER 3: INTIMATE

Day 1: Read John 14. What do you learn about Jesus and his relationship with the Father?

Day 2: Read John 15. What do you learn about Jesus and his relationship with the Father?

Day 3: Read John 16. What do you learn about Jesus and his relationship with the Father?

Day 4: Read John 17. What do you learn about Jesus and his relationship with the Father?

Day 5: Read Jeremiah 33:3. Prayer is conversation with God. Select a psalm and pray it back to God, adding your personal requests and concerns. Or pray using this acrostic of FACTS:

First, listen to God. Start your prayer time by saying, "God, you go first." Quietly wait for what he brings to your mind, and pray about each subject. When we allow God to go first, critical issues will come to the surface and God will point out areas that he would like to address.

Adoration: Praise God for who he is, his attributes, traits and qualities.

Confession: Be quiet and ask God to point out any areas of sin standing between you and him. Agree with God when he points out the sin, and thank him for his forgiveness and love.

Thanksgiving: Thank God for his great works and answered prayers, and count your many blessings.

Supplication: Name your prayer requests. Intercede for others who have needs.

Weekend: Read James 4:7-10. Think of several women who have a close relationship with Christ. Ask them what resources they use for Bible study and daily devotions.

CHAPTER 4: IDEALISTIC

Day 1: Read the following Scriptures and write what each one teaches you about how God sees you:

Matthew 5:13-16
1 Corinthians 3:16-17
Ephesians 1:1-14
Colossians 2:6-12
1 Peter 2:9-12

Which of the Scripture passages encourages you most, and why?

Day 2: Read Psalm 139. What new insights do you gain about God? Select a favorite verse from Psalm 139 and memorize it.

Day 3: Read Isaiah 40:12-31. Compare the problems of your life with the greatness of God. Bring your problems to him in prayer.

Day 4: Read John 1:1-18. Write your thoughts about the greatness and the sufficiency of Christ.

Day 5: Read Romans 11:33-36; Ephesians 3:20; Colossians 1:15-20. Say these Scriptures out loud to the Lord.

Weekend: List your weaknesses paired with their opposites—God's strengths. Find Scriptures about the strengths of God. String them together into a love letter from God's heart to yours (see my sample in chapter four).

Create your own personalized altar or reminder of how big God is. If you are willing, bring it to your group meeting next week.

CHAPTER 5: INTERDEPENDENT

Day 1: Read 2 Timothy 2:1-2 and Titus 2:1-8. What do you learn about mentoring/discipleship relationships? Who are you mentoring? Who is mentoring you?

Day 2: Read Luke 5:17-26. Faithful stretcher-bearer friends brought the paralyzed man to Jesus. Jesus healed him and complimented the friends' faith (v. 20). Who are your stretcher-bearer friends? Send thank-you notes to those whom you would call if you found yourself in tough circumstances.

Day 3: Read Matthew 28:18-20 and Acts 1:6-11. What relationships do you have with those who do not yet know Jesus? Make a list of about ten of those people and begin to pray regularly for them.

Day 4: Read 2 Timothy 4:1-8. Whom do you cheer on in life? Who cheers you on? Find a way to thank your cheerleaders today.

Day 5: Read John 3:1-15. Nicodemus sought out Jesus. Make an appointment today with someone you think of as a spiritual mentor or leader. Make plans to spend time with her and do something to encourage her.

Weekend: Women of influence have a network of friends and colleagues who help and encourage women. Begin a file of resources for the women God brings across your path, including Christian counselors; directors of women's ministries and others in the people-helping field; domestic violence shelters; food banks; financial counselors, and so on.

CHAPTER 6: INITIATIVE

Day 1: Take a long-range goal and run it through the S.T.E.P. staircase. As the week progresses, identify the steps you need and begin to create a plan to accomplish your goal.

Sometimes it is difficult to discern whether a plan is God's idea or your own. Identify a decision with which you are struggling. To find guidance, read the following Scriptures and ask yourself these questions:

Proverbs 12:15 and 15:22. Have I sought godly counsel about this? What are wise people telling me about it?

James 4:13-17. Have I surrendered my plans to God?

Romans 12:3-8; 1 Corinthians 12:1-11. Does the plan make best use of my gifts?

Day 2: Continue to work on your S.T.E.P. plan. Take time to pray over it. Look for obstacles you need to overcome and information you need to gather.

Read the following Scriptures about guidance and answer the questions about your plan:

1 Thessalonians 4:1. Will my plan help me to live more and more in a way that pleases God?

Romans 14:22-23. Does the plan require faith?

Day 3: Continue to work on your S.T.E.P. plan. Take time to pray over it.

Read 1 Chronicles 28. Is there a possibility that my plan will be completed only by a future generation? How do I react to such a possibility?

Day 4: Proverbs 16:1, 3, 9; 19:21. Are my desires the same as God's? If not, do I want them to be?

Day 5: 2 Corinthians 1:12-22. Am I resisting the urge to make my plans in a worldly manner, letting the world affect my thinking?

Colossians 3:15. Do I have peace about this decision?

Weekend: Write down seven-year goals, one-year goals and six-month goals.

Seven-year goals:

    Spiritual:

    Team:

    Energy:

    Productivity:

One-year goals:

    Spiritual:

    Team:

    Energy:

    Productivity:

Six-month goals (place these on your calendar):

    Spiritual:

    Team:

    Energy:

    Productivity:

CHAPTER 7: INTEGRITY

Day 1: What do the following Scriptures tell you about integrity?

    Romans 12:1-2
    Ephesians 5:1-7

Day 2: What do the following Scriptures tell you about integrity?

    Colossians 3:12-14
    1 Thessalonians 4:3-8

Day 3: What do the following Scriptures tell you about integrity?

    2 Timothy 1:8-14; 2:20-21

Day 4: What do the following Scriptures tell you about integrity?

Hebrews 12:14-17

1 Peter 1:13-17

Day 5: Select an area of your life and look up Bible passages to help you discern God's heart in that area.

Weekend: Consider whether you have a pure heart for the Lord or whether your heart is divided. Read Psalm 37. Note the characteristics and the consequences of an upright and pure heart.

CHAPTER 8: INTENSE

Day 1: Read 1 Corinthians 10:13 and James 4:7-10. How do you know if you should remain in a circumstance or flee it?

Day 2: Read Psalm 62 and Matthew 11:28-30. What do you learn about God's perspective on rest?

Day 3: Read Mark 6:30-31. Sometimes we get overwhelmed because we are carrying too many responsibilities at once. Make a list of everything for which you are responsible. What can you delegate? What can you delete? What can you postpone?

Day 4: Read Exodus 20:8 and Leviticus 23:3. Why do you think God made provision for humans to rest as well as to work?

Day 5: Read Deuteronomy 16:9-17. Celebration reduces stress because it reminds us that life has an upside! What can you celebrate before the Lord today?

Weekend: Interview some more mature Christians. What wisdom can they give you about how to be a person who carries on well until the finish line?

CHAPTER 9: INQUIRING

Day 1: Read Luke 1:5-56. What kind of relationship did Mary and

Elizabeth have? What do you think Mary gained from her relationship with her older relative?

Day 2: Read 1 Thessalonians 2:1-12. How do you feel about helping someone else grow in her faith? What do you learn from the model demonstrated in this passage?

Day 3: Read Philippians 2:19-30. What do you learn from Paul's relationships with Timothy and Epaphroditus?

Day 4: Read Mark 6:7-12 and Luke 9:10-17. How did Jesus stretch the faith and understanding of his disciples?

Day 5: Read Matthew 26:57-75 and John 21:15-19. What do the interaction of Jesus and Peter demonstrate about a mentoring relationship?

Weekend: What changes in yourself or your life do you think God wants to make in order to best equip you to be a lifelong disciplemaker?

CHAPTER 10: INFECTIOUS

Day 1: Read Acts 4:1-12. Today show someone who is a prebeliever that you care for her.

Day 2: Read Romans 10:5-13. Buy a book that can help you answer someone's questions about God, Jesus or the Bible.

Day 3: Read 2 Peter 3:8-9. Post a list of prebelievers you know, and commit yourself to pray daily for them and for an opportunity to share Jesus with them.

Day 4: Read 1 Peter 3:13-16. Where do you need to display more "gentleness and respect" toward prebelievers?

Day 5: Read Mark 6:32-34. After church this Sunday, try asking someone these three questions:

"What did you think of church today?"

"Did the message make sense to you?" (Or "What did you appreciate in the message?")

"Would you like to know more about a personal relationship with Christ?"

Weekend: Write a letter to God. Explain how you would like to see him use what you have learned to influence the world. Who are you praying will come to Christ? Who will you disciple? mentor? teach? How do you want God to turn your passion into a ministry? Tell God all about it in your letter. Seal it, address it to yourself, stamp it and ask someone trustworthy to mail it to you in six months. Now watch and see how God will use you to influence the world!

Bonus Section 2

SMALL GROUP DISCUSSION GUIDE

*T*his guide for small group meetings can be adapted for a one-on-one discipleship or mentoring relationship. Before each meeting, participants should read the chapter and complete the "Living It Out" section at the end of the chapter. There are also "Living It Each Day" devotions in Bonus Section 1 for each participant to do on her own. The leader may have participants do the daily quiet times the week before or the week following the small group meeting.

In the pages that follow under each chapter title you will find three elements for your small group meeting:

• an icebreaker opening section

• chapter discussion questions for the small group meeting

• a closing, which wraps up the session with prayer and commitment

Instructions for the group leader are in *italics*.

CHAPTER 1
A Woman of Influence Is Impassioned

OPENING

What is one positive thing you learned from your mother?

Other than your mother, who are the women who have most influenced your life?

CHAPTER DISCUSSION

1. Chapter one includes stories of several women. Which one(s) did you identify with most, and why?

2. Find a partner and share your answers to these questions:

   When your home is quiet, where do your daydreams take you?
   What makes you righteously angry or brings you to tears?
   What do you think you talk about the most?
   What or who are you willing to die for?
   Who or what principles would you go to jail for?
   Who are you willing to be inconvenienced for?

3. Regather the group. Have each participant write her name on a slip of paper and put it in a hat or other container. Have each participant draw a name; if she gets her own, she should put it back and draw another.

Complete this statement for the person whose name you drew: "When I think of _____(name)_____, I think of _____(some strength or ability)_____, and I appreciate that attribute because _____."

If group members are new to each other, have each participant tell something she loves to do. In a given time limit, other group members call out ways God might use that ability to help another person come to know God or grow closer to God.

4. If you had unlimited funds and were guaranteed success, what would you want to do for God?

CLOSING

Have a volunteer pray over the passion that God has laid on each heart.

CHAPTER 2
A Woman of Influence Is an Individual

Have a hat available for the chapter discussion.

OPENING

Studies say that women don't see themselves as leaders until others acknowledge them as leaders and affirm their strengths. How have others complimented you on some strength of yours recently? How did you feel about the compliment(s)?

CHAPTER DISCUSSION

Pass the hat around and ask each person to wear it while answering both parts of question 1.

1. If you took the leadership style test on pages 35-38, what did you discover about your leadership style? Where do you think your style of leadership would be most effective?

2. Read John 15:15-17. What does Jesus ask of his followers? What does he promise his followers? How do his words encourage you?

3. Respond to this survey:

   a. The age groups I like to work with best are: (name three)

   b. I prefer to: (choose one)

   __ work alone

   __ work independently but be part of a team

   __ work as a team

   __ work as the boss of a team

   c. I love work or ministry best at this stage: (choose one)

   __ the dream, when everything is still in its planning stage

   __ the ground floor, when the foundation is being laid

   __ the well-oiled machine, when most of the kinks are gone and there is a smooth, predictable system

__ regrouping, when problem-solving or new ideas are needed

d. I prefer to be accountable for growth to: (choose one)

__ one other person

__ small group of 2-3

__ small group of 4-10

__ large group of more than 10

e. I like being in charge of or responsible for: (choose one)

__ no one

__ one other person

__ small group of less than 5

__ medium group of 6-20

__ large group of over 20

__ large group of over 50

__ the larger the better

4. What do you think you need to overcome in order to see yourself as a woman of influence?

CLOSING

Pray for the woman on your right, along these lines: that she will see herself as God sees her, value herself and her leadership style, and step out to use her leadership style.

CHAPTER 3
A Woman of Influence Is Intimate with God

Ask group members to bring as many of their own Bible study resources as possible. Consider a field trip to a Christian bookstore to investigate Bible study resources; if there is a coffee shop on the premises or nearby, consider holding this meeting there. Be prepared to let group members in on how you conduct your own devotional times and any struggles and victories you have experienced in your commitment to a daily quiet time. Consider giving a copy of your favorite devotional or Bible study resource to someone you influence, and include a note explaining why you find it valuable.

OPENING

Think of a good friend. What did you do that developed and strengthened your relationship?

CHAPTER DISCUSSION

1. Give an example of how your daily time with the Lord has particularly helped you. Be as specific as possible.

2. Read Mark 1:32-35. What do you learn about how Christ gained wisdom and strength for life?

3. Where is your favorite place to spend time with the Lord, and why?

4. What is your biggest obstacle to a regular personal time with the Lord?

Give group members the opportunity to tell about their favorite Bible study resources and to practice using various resources.

5. What is one Bible study resource you learned about that you would like to use to help you understand the Bible better?

6. Read over the quiet time ideas at the end of chapter three. Which one would you like to try this week?

7. You will be more consistent at spending time with Jesus if you have a regular time and place to meet him. Find a partner and tell each other where and when you will meet with God daily.

CLOSING

Instead of each person sharing prayer requests and then praying, have each person pray for her own request, then have another group member pray over that person.

CHAPTER 4
A Woman of Influence Is Idealistic

OPENING

Do you think it is possible to be both an idealist and a realist? Explain your answer.

CHAPTER DISCUSSION

1. When are you most likely to forget who God is?

2. To live out a big view of God, we can exchange our weaknesses and fears for God's strengths. What is one weakness or fear you have right now? What is its opposite? (Examples: anger/joy; anxiety/peace.)

3. What is your scariest place of ministry or type of ministry?

4. Read Psalm 46. List the various ways that God is described as helping us.

5. What trait of God would help you battle down your fear? (For example, do you need a shield, a shepherd, a father, a fortress, etc.?)

6. To what extent do you model a big view of God to those in your sphere of influence (your family, friends, coworkers, those you are discipling, etc.)?

7. What one habit or behavior do you think God wants you to start or stop so those in your realm of influence can gain a bigger view of God?

8. Talk about Project Esther from chapter four. Discuss how you will either (1) each have your own individual Project Esther party or (2) host a Project Esther party as a group. Select a date at least eight weeks after the conclusion of your *Woman of Influence* study. Set a date for a planning session, perhaps as a "Session 11" one week after your final *Woman of Influence* session.

CLOSING

Begin your prayer time by worshiping God for who he is. Pray for your Project Esther outreach plans. Also take time to thank God for each group member's talents, gifts and possibilities.

CHAPTER 5
A Woman of Influence Is Interdependent

Group members may have brought their personalized reminders of how big God is (see last week's "Weekend" in Bonus Section 1). Ask if anyone has brought her personal reminder or wants to describe it if she was not able to bring it.

OPENING

Whose encouraging words or words of correction turned the path of your life for the better? What did the person say or do that made such a difference in your life?

CHAPTER DISCUSSION

1. What did you learn from chapter five that might help you extend God's love to people you find difficult to love?

2. In chapter five, Pam mentioned several different kinds of relationships: mentor, mentee (someone for whom you are a mentor), stretcher-bearer, prebeliever, cheerleader (encourager). Which of these do you lack and need to search for?

3. Read Acts 20:13-38. How did Paul handle his farewell to the elders of Ephesus?

4. How can you apply Paul's example to your own life concerning people it is time to let out of your life?

5. Jesus had many followers, but he had only twelve disciples and only three in his inner circle (Peter, James and John). How do you decide who gets the most access to you, your time and your life?

CLOSING

Pray for each other, especially about one relationship where you would like to see God intervene and work.

To encourage an ongoing connection among group members, take time after prayer to begin to plan a group celebration for the conclusion of this study, such as going on an overnight trip, attending a conference together, having a tea or enjoying some other special event. Allow time at this event for each member of the group to affirm the others.

CHAPTER 6
A Woman of Influence Takes Initiative

OPENING

What is one thing you would like said about you at your funeral?

CHAPTER DISCUSSION

1. Find a partner. Ask each other, "Who is one woman you know

that has set a goal and accomplished it? What are some of the steps she took to get there?"

2. Read Ephesians 5:8-20. What do you learn about setting goals that fit with God's priorities?

3. What challenges do you face in setting goals when your life is closely entwined with others (husband, parents, children, etc.)?

4. Find a different partner than you had for question one. Share a goal you have in each of these areas:

  Spiritual (a goal to get you closer to God)
  Team (a goal that builds into someone you love)
  Energy (a goal to take better care of yourself)
  Productivity (a goal to help you move forward in work,
    ministry, home, finances or education)

5. Using the S.T.E.P. diagram from page 111, write your goals in sequence on each step on the staircase. If you are willing, share them with the group.

CLOSING

Pray for the woman on your right for wisdom in goal setting and for God's will to be done as she moves forward toward her goals.

CHAPTER 7
A Woman of Influence Has Integrity

OPENING

What motto or saying has helped you make wise choices (for example, "If in doubt, don't")?

As a leader I sometimes look for small gifts to remind women to walk in integrity. For this lesson I always give a small turtle to each woman to remind them that "if you see a turtle on a post, you know it didn't get there by itself." I tell them, "God has placed you in a position of influence, but he can also take you off that platform of ministry. Keep this turtle on your desk to remind yourself to humble yourself under the mighty hand of God and he will exalt you."

CHAPTER DISCUSSION

1. To what extent do you feel the pressure of others observing your life as a woman of influence?

2. In which gray areas do you have the hardest time discerning whether or not to do something?

3. Read 1 Corinthians 10:23—11:1. What principles do you glean for behaving with integrity?

4. Why do you think integrity is the most looked for and appreciated trait people want in their leaders?

5. Josh McDowell created a necklace to help his daughter make wise choices. On the necklace are three hearts with three question marks, symbolizing three questions to ask before any choice: "Does this show love for God? Love for others? Love for self?" What decision would those three questions help you with this week?

6. One way to decide if an action is right is to ask yourself how it matches up with the character of God. Voice one area of life where you are trying to figure out God's will, and invite the rest of the group to link it to some aspect of the character of God.

CLOSING

Pray for wisdom and integrity in every decision.

CHAPTER 8
A Woman of Influence Is Intense

OPENING
How do you decide when you are "too busy"?

CHAPTER DISCUSSION

1. Isaiah 26:3 says, "Thou wilt keep him in perfect peace, whose mind is stayed on thee: because he trusteth in thee" (KJV). How do you keep your mind stayed on the Lord?

2. Recall the words of Jill Briscoe's Cambodian translator: "You in the West, when trouble comes, say, get this off my back, God. We in the East say, strengthen my back to bear it, God." What has helped you keep going when you are tired, or stick to a task long after the feeling for it has left?

3. Read 2 Corinthians 4:7-12. Which of Paul's descriptive phrases speaks to you most personally, and why?

4. Read Hebrews 12:1-3. What keeps us from losing heart?

5. One Scriptural word for *endure* means "to remain under." When have you willingly remained under a tough circumstance?

6. How can Christian women help each other avoid burnout?

CLOSING

Find a partner and pray together about stresses you are under right now.

CHAPTER 9
A Woman of Influence Is Inquiring

OPENING

What is one adventure you would like to make sure you have before you die?

CHAPTER DISCUSSION

1. In what area(s) of life do you feel in a rut?

2. It is easier to get out and stay out of a rut when we grasp God's view of life. Read the following verses and discuss what you believe is the main point of each.

   - Matthew 28:18-20
   - 1 Thessalonians 2:7-8
   - 2 Timothy 2:2
   - Titus 2:3-5

3. Who challenges you to grow spiritually?

4. How can you make more time under that person's sphere of influence?

5. There are many ways to grow: through experience, being in a small group, being mentored, being a mentor or leader. Which way do you think would help you grow the most as the next step?

6. Choose one of the areas below. How would you like to grow in that area?

   Intellectual/educational
   Social
   Recreational/hobby

Personal spiritual growth/personal ministry

Physical/emotional

7. What is one step you can take to strengthen your influence?

8. To whom would you like to pass the baton of influence?

CLOSING

Pray that you will discover what woman of influence God would want you to disciple and mentor into a leader. Begin to pray for that woman, or pray that God shows you what woman or women to challenge to be in a Woman of Influence *study with you some time in the next year.*

CHAPTER 10
A Woman of Influence Is Infectious

OPENING

Where and when do you feel most prepared to share your faith? least prepared?

CHAPTER DISCUSSION

1. Did you come to Christ through a relationship with someone? If so, how did it happen? How did the person build a relationship

with you that made a difference in your life?

2. Read Acts 1:6-8. What would you say is your Jerusalem? your Judea and Samaria? your "ends of the earth"?

3. Read 2 Timothy 4:1-2. What are some places where you can meet and befriend those who need to come to faith in Christ? Name as many as possible.

4. How can you strengthen relationships with the prebelievers in your sphere of influence?

5. If you have personally led someone to Christ or have been on a mission trip, briefly share your experience.

6. As a group, how can you use your time, talent or treasure to reach out to people who need Jesus? See how many options, groups and ministry ideas you can come up with. Decide on one project or avenue of service you will do together in this next week.

7. If something were chiseled into granite saying what you did for the Lord, what would you want written there?

CLOSING

As a group, pray for your impact on the lost world. Close with the prayer, "Lord, impassion my heart. Here I am, Lord, use me."

NOTES

Chapter 1: Impassioned

page 12   "I could not sleep": Ruth Tucker and Walter Liefeld, *Daughters of the Church* (Grand Rapids: Zondervan/Academie Books, 1987), p. 320.

page 17   According to the Indian Ministry: Accessed at http://www.islam online.net/English/family/2005/11/article05.shtml.

page 17   Each year two million girls: Accessed at http://www.unicef.org/ protection/index_25032.html.

page 17   In developing countries: Accessed at http://www.popcouncil.org/ gfd/girlseducation.html.

page 17   Studies have shown that: Accessed online on March 9, 2006, at http://www.unicef.org/sowc96/ngirls.htm.

page 17   Between 1970 and 2003: Accessed online on March 9, 2006, at http://www.cdc.gov/nchs/data/hus/tables/2003/03hus009.pdf.

page 17   Teen suicide rose 200 percent: William Bennett, *Index of Leading Cultural Indicators* (Washington, D.C.: Heritage Foundation, March 1993), pp. i-19.

page 18   International Relief Organizations suggest: *Children of the Night: Rescuing America's Children from Prostitution*, http://www.childrenofthe night.org/faq.html.

page 18   There are approximately 200,000 women: Accessed online March 10, 2006, at http://www.oxfam.org.uk/what_we_do/where_we_work/ nepal/gender/traffic.htm.

page 18   The government of India: *Child Workers in Asia*, http://www.cwa.tnet .co.th/Publications/Newsletters/vol12_1-2/v12_1-2_factors .html.

page 18   UNICEF estimates that 1.2 million: Ibid.

page 18   George Barna did a study: George Barna, *What Americans Believe* (Ventura, Calif.: Regal, 1991), p. 179.

page 25   "If the first woman": http://www.sojournertruthhouse.com/history
                .asp.

page 26   "I would rather die than break my faith": Tucker and Liefeld, *Daughters of the Church*, p. 192.

page 26   "Don't cry, Teacher": A. Wetherell Johnson, *Created for Commitment*
                (Wheaton, Ill.: Tyndale, 1982), pp. 136-37.

pages 26-27   Perpetua was born: Tucker and Liefeld, *Daughters of the Church*, p.
                102.

page 29   "When a man takes an oath": Robert Bolt, *A Man for All Seasons*
                (New York: Vintage, 1960), p. 81.

pages 29-30   "O God, Thou puttest": Edith Deen, *Great Women of the Christian
                Faith* (New York: Harper, 1959), p. 216.

page 30   "Now I know": Ibid.

Chapter 2: Individual

page 32   "You have to be": Maureen Sajbel, "Hat Tricks," *Los Angeles Times*,
                July 14, 1994, p. E3.

page 33   "Walk like it's supposed to be there": Jennifer Levitz, "Cancer Patients Hold Their Heads High," *Times Advocate*, August 23, 1995, p.
                A1.

pages 33-34   Sally Helgesen kept a diary: Sally Helgesen, *The Female Advantage:
                Women's Ways of Leadership* (New York: Doubleday, 1990), pp. 19-28.

page 33   One study showed that women: Gary N. Powell, *Women and Men in
                Management* (Newbury Park, Calif.: Sage, 1993), p. 167.

pages 33-34   However, men *and* women: Ibid., p. 84.

page 34   Most important, men had a better ability: See Powell, *Women and
                Men in Management*, p. 162, for gender differences. Several studies
                showed men's aspirations and self-perception of leadership skills as
                higher than women's (see pp. 76-79, 105-6).

page 35   When a woman has interacted: Ibid., p. 109.

page 40   Susannah Wesley had: Edith Deen, *Great Women of the Christian
                Faith* (New York: Harper, 1959).

page 42   "We can't take all God gives us": Julie A. Talerico, "Elizabeth Dole's
                Heart and Soul," *Today's Christian Woman*, July-August 1993, p. 78.

page 43   "I thought it would be easy": Johnson, *Created for Commitment*, p. 46.

page 45   "The thought of ordination": Tucker and Liefeld, *Daughters of the
                Church*, p.271.

pages 47-48   "The authority is not in a position": Anne Graham Lotz, "Women in
                Ministry," audiotape available from AnGeL Ministry, P.O. Box

31167, Raleigh, NC 27622-1167.

page 48   "The Holy Spirit decides": Jill Briscoe, "Woman Power: The Woman's Place in the Church," audiotape 0988-8, available from Telling the Truth Ministries, P.O. Box 11, Brookfield, WI 53008.

page 48   "Dr. Ruth Tucker says that the best": Ruth Tucker, in a personal conversation, Women's Ministry Symposium, March 24, 1995.

page 48   Gretchen Gaebelein Hull, in *Equal to Serve*: Gretchen Gaebelein Hull, *Equal to Serve* (Grand Rapids: Baker, 1998).

pages 49-50   "Where shall I work": Source unknown. Excerpted from *Hope for the Heart* newsletter, December 1992 (P.O. Box 7, Dallas, TX 75221).

page 50   "When we desire to abide": Fern Nichols, in a personal interview, January 9, 1995.

Chapter 3: Intimate

page 53   C. S. Lewis, the wonderful: C. S. Lewis, *The Screwtape Letters* (Old Tappan, N.J.: Revell, 1979), p. 59.

page 53   Kay Arthur, author of Precept Bible Studies: Nancy Carmichael, "Any Bush Will Do," *Virtue,* January-February 1994, p. 31.

pages 56-57   In Molly Newman and Barbara Damashek's play: Quoted in "The Quilters," *Virtue,* March-April 1991, p. 44.

page 58   "God says He doesn't": Gracia Burnham, in an interview titled "Grace in the Jungle," in *Today's Pentecostal Evangel.* Available online at http://pentecostalevangel.ag.org/conversations2003/4658_burn ham.com.

pages 58-59   Another missionary, Nancy Mankin, understands: Nancy Mankin, New Tribes Mission audiotape, March 16, 1993.

page 61   "In a deeply personal way": Carol Kent, *When I Lay My Isaac Down: Unshakable Faith in Unthinkable Circumstances,* (Colorado Springs: NavPress, 2004), p. 29.

page 62   A preschooler accidently spilled: *Today's Christian Woman,* January-February 1996, p. 25.

page 62   "I pray because": *Shadowlands,* film directed and produced by Richard Attenborough (HBO Home Video and Savoy Video, 1993). Also produced by Brian Eastman.

page 64   After twenty-four hours: *1 to 1 Discipleship Manual* (Vista, Calif.: Church Dynamics, 1983), p. 24.

pages 65-66   "You are the Rock of my salvation: Teresa Muller, "You Are the Rock of My Salvation," *Praise VII,* © 1982, Maranatha Music. Used by permission.

Chapter 4: Idealistic

page 70   "It is the individual who counts": Henrietta Mears, quoted in Earl R. Roe, *Dream Big* (Ventura, Calif.: Regal, 1990), p. 265.

page 71   "This is the most ridiculous": Henrietta Mears, quoted in ibid., p. 161.

pages 71-72   Once she said: Ibid., p. 57.

pages 73-74   *"Nothing is impossible"*: paraphrased from 1 Chronicles 29:11-12; Job 41:33; Psalm 139; Isaiah 9:6; 40; Zechariah 4:6; Matthew 17:20; Romans 8:38-40; 11:33; Ephesians 3:20; Colossians 1:16-17; 1 Timothy 6:16; Hebrews 4:16; Revelation 22:13.

page 77   The word *pledge:* R. V. J. Tasker, *The Second Epistle of Paul to the Corinthians,* Tyndale New Testament Commentaries (London: Inter-Varsity Press, 1983), 8:49.

page 77   In *Our Faithful God:* Quoted in Edith Deen, *Great Women of the Christian Faith* (New York: Harper, 1959), p. 216.

page 78   "God and one are always a majority": Mary Slessor, quoted in William Brooks, "Mary, Queen of Calabar," *Worldwide Challenge,* July-August 1994, p. 47.

page 80   On one trip: William Bennett, *The Book of Virtues* (New York: Simon & Schuster, 1993), pp. 503-4.

page 81   Believing her actions were inspired: Paul Thigpen, "Harriet Tubman: Risking Her Life to Set Others Free," *Discipleship Journal,* November-December 1994, p. 63.

Project Esther

page 85   Everybody has a unique gift to offer: If you want even more detailed information and help to discern your calling, see my book *The 10 Best Decisions A Woman Can Make,* http://farrelcommunications.com. For a sample of a gospel presentation, see pp. 81-82 of that same book.

Chapter 5: Interdependent

page 91   Linda comments: Personal e-mail interview with the author, October 27, 2005.

pages 99-100   A top-ranking British official: InfoSearch, NavPress PC Software, illustration 62.

page 101   "Amy Carmichael became for me": Elisabeth Elliot, *A Chance to Die* (Grand Rapids: Revell, 1987), p. 15.

page 103   There are "friends of the heart": Elizabeth Cody Newenhuyse, "Friendship Fizzle," *Today's Christian Woman,* January-February 1995, p. 52.

Chapter 6: Initiative

page 107   Years later she wrote in a letter: Catherine Booth, quoted in Deen, *Great Women of the Christian Faith*, p. 243.

pages 107-8   "It will be a happy day": Ibid., p. 239.

page 110   Emilie Barnes writes: Emilie Barnes, *The Creative Home Organizer* (Eugene, Ore.: Harvest House, 1988), p. 15.

page 113   Daisy Hepburn advises: Daisy Hepburn, address given at a women's conference, Pine Valley, California, March 11, 1989.

page 115   "When a house is on fire": Corrie ten Boom, *Each New Day* (Grand Rapids: Spire, 1977), p. 39.

page 119   Included at the end: Excellent financial resources are available at your local Christian bookstore. Recommended authors include Ron and Judy Blue, and Larry Burkett.

Chapter 7: Integrity

page 129   Someone who understands the principles: For more information on spiritual warfare and your identity in Christ, contact Freedom in Christ Ministries, 491 E. Lambert Rd., La Habra, CA 90631. Phone (310) 691-9128.

Page 135   She says, "My parents had me absolutely convinced": Condoleezza Rice, quoted in Antonia Felix, *Condi* (Grand Rapids: Zondervan, 2005), p. 36.

pages 135-36   She says "When I'm concerned": B. Denise Hawkins, "Condoleezza Rice's Secret Weapon: How Our National Security Adviser Finds the Strength to Defend the Free World," *Christian Reader,* September-October 2002. Accessible at http://www.christianitytoday.com/tc/2002/005/1.18.html.

Chapter 8: Intense

pages 138-39   "My feet were swollen": Gail Devers, quoted in Kenny Moore, "Dash to Glory," *Sports Illustrated,* August 10, 1992, p.18.

page 139   "I felt I was washed up": Gail Devers, quoted in "Devers Overcomes Ailments to Dash for Olympic Gold," *Jet,* August 17, 1992, p. 51.

page 139   Bob Kersee embraced: Quoted in Moore, "Dash to Glory," p. 19.

pages 139-40   Later Gail told the press: Gail Devers, quoted in "Devers Overcomes Ailments," p. 51.

page 141   A poster of Heather: Deniese George, "Capturing a Nation's Heart," *Pursuit* 11, no. 4, p. 26.

page 141   "We are all worthy to Him": Ibid., p. 30.

page 141   "My crown should erase the word 'impossible'": "Heather White-stone," *People,* December 26, 1994, p. 122.

page 142   The speaker compared women to boats: Jill Briscoe, "Running on Empty" audiotape, 1991 National Conference for Ministry Wives, Orlando, Fla., February 19-21, 1991.

page 142   Businesswoman Mary Kay Ash: Mary Kay Ash, quoted in Neil Taylor, *How to Lose 10 Pounds* (Nashville: Nelson, 1993), p. 37.

page 143   She declared to the judge: Susan B. Anthony, quoted in Deen, *Great Women of the Christian Faith*, p. 78.

page 144   The Cambodian woman: Jill Briscoe, Newim Conference, Arrowhead Springs, Calif., June 2, 1994.

page 148   We should never doubt in the darkness: Neil Anderson, Freedom in Christ Seminar, San Diego, Calif., July 1994.

page 150   Eating pure food the way God made it: Stormie Omartian, *Greater Health God's Way* (Chatsworth, Calif.: Sparrow, 1984), p. 52.

Chapter 9: Inquiring

page 155   When Chuck Colson went: Quoted in Charles Colson, *Loving God* (Grand Rapids: Zondervan, 1983), pp. 209-16.

page 155   When a mother eagle: InfoSearch, illustration 109.

page 155   Oscar Wilde said: Quoted in Charlie Jones and Bob Phillips, *Wit and Wisdom* (Eugene, Ore.: Harvest House, 1977), p. 52.

Chapter 10: Infectious

page 169   Cynthia says, "I had to learn": Cynthia McKinney, in a personal interview, December 12, 1994.

page 170   In 2004 over 2 million teenagers: Accessed March 10, 2006, at http://www.syatp.com/media/journalists/press_release.html.

page 176   She says "Jesus illustrates": Quoted in Monica Whiting, "Living Christ and Gabbing over Lunch," *Discipleship Journal,* September-October 1994, p. 41.

pages 181-82   Kay describes her reaction: Kay Cole James, *Never Forget* (Grand Rapids: Zondervan, 1992), p. 159.

page 182   Her mother replied: Ibid., p. 169.

page 183   "One cannot transform": Robert Coleman, *The Master Plan of Evangelism* (Old Tappan, N.J.: Spire, 1978), p. 24.

ABOUT THE AUTHOR

*P*am Farrel is an international speaker and bestselling author of nearly thirty books, including *Men Are like Waffles, Women Are like Spaghetti; Love, Honor and Forgive; The One Year Book of Devotions for Women on the Go; The 10 Best Decisions Every Parent Can Make* and *The 10 Best Decisions a Woman Can Make.* She has experience as a director of women, radio host, pastor's wife, women's conference speaker and mentor of women for over twenty-five years. She has been happily married to her husband, Bill, for over twenty-six years, and together they enjoy speaking on marriage and family issues. Pam is also a mother of three and enjoys spending time with her new daughter-in-law.

You can contact Pam at

Farrel Communications
P. O. Box 1507
San Marcos, CA 92079
800-810-4449
www.farrelcommunications.com